The Signs and Wonders Movement –EXPOSED

Mark Haville

Chris Hand

Philip Foster

Peter Glover

Editor: Peter Glover

DayOne

First printed 1997

Scripture quotations are taken from The New King James Version

ISBN 0902 548 751

Published by Day One Publications
6 Sherman Road, Bromley, Kent BR1 3JH

Designed by Steve Devane and printed by Clifford Frost Ltd, Wimbledon SW19 2SE

"It is more to God's glory that the world should be conquered by the force of truth than by the blaze of miracles." **Charles Spurgeon**

"...the degree of grace is by no means to be judged by the degree of joy, or the degree of zeal......it is not the degree of religious affections but the nature of them that is chiefly to be looked at."

"..we are to take the Scriptures as our guide in such cases. This is the great and standing rule which God has given to His Church......it is an infallible and sufficient rule. There are undoubtedly sufficient marks given to guide the Church of God in this great affair of judging the spirits, without which it would lie open to woeful delusion."

The Distinguishing Marks of a Work of the True Spirit **Jonathan Edwards**

The Signs and Wonders Movement –EXPOSED

True Christianity, throughout its two thousand years, has been plagued with a succession of false movements, false prophets and false teachers. We should not be surprised that it should be so – Jesus and the apostles warned us often enough. But, what all Christians should remember is that the heresies of these groups and individuals did not try to invade the Church from the outside – they arose from within it.

Why did they succeed in gaining acceptance? Because they appeared 'spiritual'. They appeared to provide a 'deeper' knowledge, a 'truer' understanding of the gospel. There have always been those in the Church's history who claimed or appeared to have a private hotline to God. Through their own personal and private revelation, they would distil true spirituality – faith in Christ and the obeying of God's Word – into super-spiritual and sensual forms of experiential, liberal or legalistic Christianity.

Many Christians today are completely unaware of the history of their own Church. They are ignorant of the Church battles with mystical Christian groups and individuals: Gnosticism, Montanism, the teaching of Tertullian, the French Prophets, the Anabaptists and so on. They know little of unorthodox (ie: non-biblical) and heretical forms of belief and teaching that have struck at the heart of the true gospel. The apostle Paul was clear-sighted in his spiritual discernment. He called such belief 'a different gospel – which is really no gospel at all'. He did so because it always depicted a distorted Jesus and a distorted gospel message.

The movements themselves often caused the Church to look again at its own foundation set on the firm ground of the teaching of Jesus and the apostles. In doing so, the Church was able to protect itself against these aberrations of true spirituality. It was able increasingly to define truth by reference only to God's own self-revelation to us – *those taught and written down for us in our Bible*. The teaching of our Lord and the apostles – the authoritative word of Scripture *alone* – has been the only protection against every deception and heresy that has assailed the Church in every generation since Christ walked the earth.

The Scriptures, brought alive to us by the gift of the Holy Spirit through faith, enabled Luther to stand against the political and religious tyranny of a deceived (Roman Catholic) Church. They enabled Wesley, Whitefield, Edwards and thousands of others to reach hearts and minds with the living gospel. It allowed the common man to know the closeness of a loving God and Father and to know when he was being peddled something counterfeit. There was no hidden, deeper, mystical, secret message when it came to the gospel – Jesus and the apostles had seen to that.

In common with many other faiths, cults, religions and belief–systems, many in today's Church are, once again, abandoning the Word for the 'higher and deeper' spiritual world. As we approach the third millennium men and women, in today's Church, are once again becoming drawn to degrees of Gnostic (Greek *gnosis*: higher knowledge) and mystical belief.

We have come full circle. Gnosticism – the very reason for the existence of some of our New Testament books – was a first century heresy. It has returned with a vengeance and is sweeping the Church, including the former bastion of *sola scriptura*, (the Reformers reference to the authority of Scripture *alone*) the Evangelical Church. Many have fallen for the age old heresy of believing the Holy Spirit operates independently from God's spoken Word. There is nothing new in this separation of Word from Spirit. The Reformation was a response to growing unbiblical practice inside the Church. For many, Church and society before the Reformers came on the scene, mirrors Church and society in our own day. What *is* new in our day, however, is that the bastion of *sola scriptura* itself, Evangelicalism, is itself being seduced away from the Word of God as the only authority for belief and practice in the Church.

The purpose of this book is to look at just one such movement, but one which sustains, underpins and feeds so many others – the modern Signs & Wonders Movement. This Movement and it's adherents straddle the breadth of Christian belief and Church background. The names of some of it's proponents are familiar enough as the very nature of their claims and practices feeds the voracious appetite of the media for entertainment and the spectacular. Their names are soon up in lights often bringing fame and, most significantly, very large personal fortune with it.

In the rush to 'be like them' thousands upon thousands are departing their Scriptural heritage – God's eternal Word. The players in our age include: Kenneth Copeland, John Wimber, Benny Hinn, Morris Cerullo, John Arnott, Colin Dye, Gerald Coates, Terry Virgo and many, many others. We could just as easily list them with Montanus, Tertullian and James Davenport (to whom Jonathan Edwards apportioned much blame for, in his 'Spirit-led' zeal, destroying a true revival of God). Their zeal also caused them to depart the true Word. They too believed they were led by the Holy Spirit alone and received private revelation direct from God. At least Davenport repented his excesses in tears. Praise be to God that even spiritual deception can be temporary.

Many contemporary exponents are referred to in these pages. Some are extremely 'nice', charming individuals. It makes not a jot of difference. Only one question really matters: *Is what they teach true?* Far too many believe it is 'true' because they 'see something supernatural happen'. What they do not realise is that supernatural manifestations prove nothing – and they can come from two sources, not one. Therefore they require close examination (spiritual discernment) by the only microscope given us by God himself – His own Word.

In gross ignorance many Christians today are unaware that the devil does not mind doing apparent 'good' or performing supernatural tricks to enthral and mystify, if he can achieve his *real* objective – *shielding us from God's truth*. They have forgotten that we are all too easily drawn to the unusual and mysterious. That is why when the crowds got too big, Jesus usually moved on – He knew they wanted to see him perform. Jesus knew only too well that performing tricks obscured the message. His signs and wonders were only done in conjunction with the proclamation of a message of truth – *in His own sovereign time.*

Everybody loves a show and we can all be taken in by anything that we cannot understand. That is how hypnotist Paul McKenna and illusionist David Copperfield make their living. Neither, however, are revealers of truth (neither do they claim to be) – both obscure it. We are all too easily seduced into a credulous state of gullibility. God knew it and realised that what we needed was objective truth that allows us to weigh and test even the supernatural. *If you are one of those who is questioning current phenomena and is seriously wanting to know 'If it is not God – then what is happening?' – this book is for you.*

In the current climate, as many trample over the eternal truths of Scripture, the doctrines of our faith, in pursuit of what they believe to be first-hand experience of the Holy Spirit, some Christians are in complete ignorance that it has all happened before. The Bible is as clear as it is possible to be in warning us of the 'wiles of the devil', not least, his ability to duplicate signs and wonders. And yet, so many Christians are still prepared to label almost any supernatural occurrence as 'of the Spirit of God'. But experience has always been a poor substitute for practical faith because, by definition, it is subjective. That is why experience/ power encounters have always been of little value in the real spiritual battle.

Spiritual discernment in the Church today is at an all-time low. Most modern day Christians do not even know what this gift is or how it can be gained. In such a climate spiritual deception can only flourish. Yet, here again, many Christians seem to believe that spiritual discernment is a gift in the mystical realm, to which only a few have access. Nothing could be further from the truth. Spiritual discernment comes with knowledge of God's Word and a 'right using of that Word'. The *only* test we have is Scripture. With it we are truly equipped to deal with false teaching – without it we are sitting ducks waiting to be 'suckered' by the latest spiritual counterfeit that comes our way.

Add to this the fact that too many Christians are now prepared to hand over responsibility for their Christian walk to authoritative, 'anointed' leaders (usually signs & wonders performers – surely, many say, they must have a closer walk with God!), and we have a recipe for spiritual deception on a massive scale. We have become sensual Christians, deserving once again of Jesus' rebuke for seeking a sign, some physical (in the guise of spiritual) assurance that 'God is there'. We have God's Word and our faith rests on it.

In the sixteenth century the Reformers knew this: faith *alone*, scripture *alone*, Christ *alone* was written on their banner – and it turned both Church and society around. How many times must we learn: we live by faith – *not by sight*. For *sight*, read experience.

This book is an attempt to redress the balance. Whatever your Church background, it is our hope that the collective experience contained in these pages will help you understand that it is not the 'blowing wind' of Pentecost from which our faith stems, but from the 'dripping blood' of Calvary. Many, perhaps confused by what they are witnessing in an increasingly experience-orientated atmosphere in the modern Church may be looking for firm ground. It is our hope you may find it, not just here in these pages, but in the pages of God's Word written, towards which this book points.

The writers all emanate from very different Church backgrounds:

Mark Haville is Director of the National Prayer Network. He has an important story to tell. He has personally known or been in association with many of the big-name performers in today's Signs & Wonders Movement. To my knowledge Mark is the only Word-Faith Minister and worker of modern signs and wonders to repent of these works. His message is simple but vital – what passes for signs and wonders today is a learned process. He did it, you could do it, anyone could do it.

Chris Hand, is Pastor at Grace Baptist Church, Lewisham in South London. He would now describe himself as of a reformed evangelical position. But, in 1995, he was Assistant Pastor at Queens Road Baptist Church in Wimbledon, England, a charismatic Church at the heart of things when the Toronto Blessing (the most visible recent outworking of the Signs & Wonders Movement) came to Britain. For a whole summer he observed the Toronto-Experience phenomena transform his Church. He has a powerful message for all those who are genuinely interested in the much-vaunted fruit of Toronto. Chris is a co-founder of Christian Research Network which researches beliefs and practices in contemporary Christianity.

Philip Foster is an Anglican Minister at St Matthews in Cambridge. Philip would describe himself as charismatic. Over many years he has researched and written on the subject of new movements within the Church and has hosted a conference on the subject. His pastor's heart has given him a penchant to protect the flock from spiritual deception. To this end he has worked to bring together much evidence on the power of hypnotism and suggestibility and its links to modern movements within the Church.

Peter Glover is an Anglican Lay Reader and leader of a Church-plant, part of St Luke's, West Norwood in South London and would describe himself as being of a reformed evangelical position. Peter is a co-founder of Christian Research Network which researches beliefs and practices in contemporary Christianity. He is a Public Relations Consultant and freelance journalist writing on Christian belief and practice, new religious movements and on social issues.
It is our joint hope that Christians will return to the Word of God as it is enlightened by the Spirit of God. It is our only hope in the present and future battle against the spiritual counterfeit that is no longer at our door – it is roaming the house in which we live.

Peter Glover
January 1997

An illusion of power

Mark Haville

It is my favourite part in the movie. I am sitting cosily on the couch with my wife Melanie. We are comfortable and close and the romantic film is coming to its climax. It is the part where Tom Hanks and his disappointed son have just left the viewing post on top of the Empire State Building. The lift on the right closes and begins its slow decent. Just at that point the other lift arrives and opens revealing Meg Ryan staring disappointedly at a vacant floorspace. She steps out to look around and ponders what might have been.

Soft background music reflectively portrays the mood and Meg Ryan's disappointment is almost tangible. Then suddenly she finds the boy's bag by the telescope and breaks into the kind of summery smile that could melt an iceberg.

She looks up just as the doors open again and Sam and Jonah look out from the lift. In a stunned silence they step towards her. It's electric. You could cut the atmosphere with a knife – while passing the tissues with the other hand! Anyway, I love it. It doesn't matter if it's only movie-magic, it brings a happy tear to my eyes and I hug my wife. We both laugh at each other for being sentimental hopefuls for the 'mush-attack-of-the-year' award! Anyway, who cares if it's based on a true story or not.

Sleepless in the battle

Our brains, for the most part, don't rationalise everything that way. We easily allow ourselves to be engaged by something that will give us an emotional buzz. After all it is enjoyable and harmless and reflects the incredible intricacy that is part of our human make-up. Fortunately, we know it is not reality. Unfortunately, I wish my thoughts on what is happening in today's Church - the lack of reality checks - could radiate the same warmth as the film *Sleepless In Seattle*. Instead they are reflected more in the title of another film - *Clear And Present Danger*.

Have you ever wondered why we react so emotionally to things we know are not real? Think about it for a moment. We can cry, shake, perspire, laugh, become tense, afraid and even sleepless over things we watch. The reason is that, temporarily at least, we allow ourselves to believe they are real. Others, of course, don't allow themselves to suspend reality and do not experience the emotions of those who do. Psychotherapists would call this a 'reality check'.

My part in this book is to highlight the need for a 'reality check' in the Christian walk of all of us in today's Church - much as I have had to do in my own. The world of *Sleepless In Seattle* is not far removed from those who are sleepless and at ease in the Church today, at a time when the biggest 'reality check' ever is needed.

Whether we cringe at a film's man-eating monster or jump when the psycho stabs his victim in a quiet lane, we all occasionally allow ourselves to be fooled by something that is not real. By something that is not based on objective truth. Equally, it is possible for our emotions to drive us like sleepwalkers, causing us to be unconscious to the reality of God's Word. All too easily we can become the servants of our emotions.

First, let me tell you something of my own spiritual journey. I do so because I believe the route I have taken is particularly relevant in the current climate of sensual, experiential Christianity sweeping the Church today. I hope, for those reading my story, it will reveal some answers to questions about which you may already have been asking yourself: truth, reality and spiritual discernment in the contemporary Church, especially as they relate to one of the most influential movements in it – the Signs and Wonders Movement.

To mention the Signs and Wonders Movement normally leads people, browsing over the first few pages of a book, to want to know where the author stands on what is commonly called the gifts of the Spirit. This may help them determine whether they will invest in the book or not. I will, therefore, briefly state my position.

I certainly believe that God through the Holy Spirit can and does manifest miracles today. But, I believe He will *only* do so as and when HE wills, not as we will.

When I first came to accept Jesus as my Lord and Saviour I joined a Pentecostal Church of sorts. During my first few years there I quickly discovered the teachings of Kenneth Copeland and other teachers in the 'health and wealth' Word-Faith Movement [1].

Unfortunately, through the influence of this Church, my first love, for the true Jesus - *the Jesus revealed in Scripture* - was quickly pushed aside by love for 'another Jesus'. This different 'Jesus' was the 'Jesus' seen through the eyes of an ancient heresy, Sabellianism (a third-century heresy suggesting there were no real distinctions in the Godhead). I was also receiving other generally unsound and distinctly unbiblical teaching. Gradually, however, real spiritual hunger pangs began to trouble me. My initial love for God, following my conversion, *should* have been carefully harnessed to a correct, biblical understanding of God, Jesus and the Holy Spirit, through the self-revelation of God's Word. Unfortunately for me, because I was not taught properly, I did not know how to discern truth from error. For me it was out of the frying pan into the fire. Because, as a result of the legalistic and of false teaching in my own Church, I found even more exciting (and heretical) teaching elsewhere.

I did not know it then, but the trouble with all false doctrine (false understanding about God) is that it can directly affect our relationship with the Lord Jesus Christ. It can also limit our faithful witness for the kingdom of God. My main problem was that I had now quickly learned to devour all the teaching I could from the world of the Faith Movement and its leading exponents, the Faith Teachers. Even through the night my auto reverse walkman played on filling my head with what I believed was God's anointed Word. Actually, they were the words of Kenneth Copeland and friends. But, for me, they were speaking as his anointed prophets and teachers. I pressed on with the teaching of Jerry Savelle, Kenneth and Gloria Copeland and Kenneth Hagin. After all, I was hungry for everything God had for me and I wanted to be everything and anything for God. I felt my faith was at a new high. I was thinking 'big'. These Christian leaders were holding the biggest crusades and they wrote best-selling books. They had offices around the globe and were alleging the most incredible miracles were taking place at their hands.

Through their tapes and books, to my way of thinking, it was obvious they were the most anointed servants of God. After all, if it wasn't true surely somebody, somewhere, would be saying something about it - wouldn't they? No one seemed to be raising much of a protest.

It was at this stage that my faith and spirituality began to fall apart. I eventually left my Church because I had begun to perceive the biblical 'unsoundness' I referred to earlier. It kept surfacing in unscriptural and unbiblical practices among the membership of the Church. All too often this was clearly reflected in a lack of integrity in practical matters.

In this condition and without the love and support of other Christians, I increasingly allowed 'worldly' problems and solutions to direct my life. I quickly backslid in my faith. Previously I had listened to Word-Faith ministry tapes for up to10 hours a day. I had read as many Word- Faith books as I could. In addition, I had attended their crusades and watched their videos.

However, when everything in my life fell apart I blamed myself and did not link any of it to my teaching. I told myself if I had been stronger and resisted sin, I would not have fallen away from God for over a year. My life was a mess. I had no fellowship and no faith. Later, my business collapsed and our house was repossessed. I subsequently got a job and began commuting to London, but I wasn't happy. I knew God had a different purpose for my life, and I thought if I ever tried to turn back to God the devil would attack me. After all, I knew I was totally in his territory, and to cap it all I now just didn't have the will to fight.

One day whilst looking out of the window these words passed across my mind "I DON'T WANT TO LIVE LIKE THIS ANYMORE". Of all men, 'backslidden' Christians are the most miserable. I had had enough. I was doing my level best to live like a sinner! I then began to spend some time with a Pastor of an exciting charismatic Church in London.

After much prayer and repentance and a renewed commitment I enrolled for a part-time Bible study course and not long after moved, with my family, to live in London. We were now all attending the new Church. I was even being groomed as a future leader by the senior Pastor. Eventually I entered the full time curriculum of the Bible college and provided assistance to help pay for my tuition.

I came across many good and sincere Christians in my Church and college who held a variety of theological beliefs, reflecting the trend of many of the larger charismatic Churches. But the common denominator, I could see, was that they all tended to base their beliefs in experience (as in sensual) Christianity. The uniting factor among most was that phenomena and experience determined belief. It was these beliefs and the underpinning teachings that I could see were drawing people to the Signs & Wonders Movement.

The King and I

The key to success as a leader on the signs and wonders circuit is the claimed 'anointing' of God on your life. My training in this area was crucial. Not only had I many thousands of hours of cassette teaching under my belt, but I had also spent time with many of the key Word-Faith and charismatic figures that they strongly influenced. I spent much time with the 'big names' themselves. I had been exposed to their ministries through their visits to my Church and through their teaching at the Bible school itself. This is where their teaching and 'imparting' were most concentrated. The students, they knew, were most likely to be future leaders. They were the key focus. They were an investment.

The way 'up' was to have such a strong presence of the Lord (an 'anointing') that, by your ministry, people around you could be changed forever. If you could 'invoke the presence of God', it seemed logical that coming into His presence would bring change. I felt I had done it all: studied, had the right contacts, experienced endless prayer, right confessions, sowing, sowing, and more sowing. At long last the King and I had really begun to minister together!

Before graduating and within the college environment I was getting more opportunity for God to use me. Some of those experiences were quite dramatic. One morning, for example, while I was leading prayer (I was intercession leader for the college) I believed the Lord told me to pray for His Spirit to fall as at Pentecost. Lessons that week had been given over to prayer and fasting. Boy did it happen! The whole school was gathered in the main hall for the entire morning. After about an hour, the place got 'hit'. People were laid out on the floor everywhere, some crying, some laughing, some having visions. Others were just praying aloud. It was incredible. The sensation was awesome. It was just as, I believed, God had 'told' me earlier that day!

After that, I was invited to speak at a number of Churches and saw equally dramatic scenes take place after the 'worship-time'. I had learned how to create the right atmosphere. I knew that the nature of the worship itself was vital to the 'anointing' falling. I knew it was essential to be personally in control of the service, to have the right songs and no distractions. I, as leader, also had to be 'primed' beforehand. It was therefore important that any personal contact I had before the service be kept to a minimum. A wrong comment, for example, could drastically affect my leading. *The atmosphere was everything.*

I knew that God needed those involved in such a service to 'feel just right' to allow the power to flow through them. The type of music also has to be just right. I knew those who only liked Christian rock would not be able to enter in with the gospel 'spirituals' and vice versa. I knew that the right music created the right ambience. Words as well, I learned, were a key element to enable us to focus on the Person of the Holy Spirit and what is going to happen. After all, did not God inhabit the praises of his people? I knew that it was during the worship it was possible to greatly build up expectation. The whole relationship between the minister and the congregation was another key factor. Those, for example, who believed that I was 'highly anointed' automatically believed that I had a greater ability to 'allow the Holy Spirit to flow' through them. If you are 'known' to be 'anointed', believers become more susceptible to phenomena than someone who has never heard of you or experienced your ministry.

In some of my services many would be helpless on the floor for half an hour or more. They would laugh, shake or maybe just speak in tongues. Some at the end of the service had to be transported home because they were unable to walk home in their own strength.

With these and other manifestations taking place the expectation for miracles (heading etc) is enormous. One characteristic trait, which was fast becoming an aspect of my own ministry, was my ability to blow on people and see them collapse onto the floor, under the 'anointing'. I knew that God himself had breathed life into Adam and he had become a living soul. Many would now collapse like dead weights when I blew. But I could also see that some did not. Perhaps they were not so open, I wondered, or maybe they were more used to the 'anointing'? Anyway I was zealous for more of God and I really wanted to see people's lives changed for the glory of God.

This, I believe, is truly the heart of many in the Signs and Wonders Movement – to be zealous for God and see lives changed. However, I could see that for all this enthusiasm, many seemed to exhibit rather obvious flaws in their lives, especially in the area of finances and in their tactics for raising funds. Such practical things had already weighed heavily on my own conscience. I was now producing the same phenomena that other leaders were producing. And yet I could clearly see that their lives, their actions and their Christian living, presented many problems. One feature was the tendency to adopt "ministerial mode". This is something the big name preachers I was copying often adopt when talking with the 'ordinary folk' after a meeting (that is the leaders who are accessible, many are not!). I often felt at such time that they were very plastic and surreal. The actions of the leaders did not to me seem in keeping with, and did not reflect, the actions and nature of our Lord Jesus. While Jesus let the little children climb on his knee and told them stories – these leaders wanted nothing to do with anyone at all, including children, when they finished ministering. Nevertheless, I pressed on.

Some of the most 'anointed' men of God were around for me to learn and receive from. I was learning financial success from Robert Tilton and Bob Harrison, passion for souls over breakfast with Morris Cerullo. I learned the 'anointing for prayer' at a private dinner with Larry Lea, 'faith' from Freddy Price and 'miracles' from Benny Hinn, Christian Harfouche and others.

I believed God was really going to use me now. I had arrived and everything was falling into place. I was on the road to fulfilling my potential and change the lives of millions in England just as Kenneth Copeland's European Director had previously prophesied over me. But, I wondered, would I be able to take the 'anointing of God' to others? That is the same anointing imparted to me by Bob Tilton, Jerry

Savelle, Larry Lea, Dick Mills and a list of others too long to remember. But now the power of the Holy Ghost was being imparted by my hands. People were 'slain', drunk in the spirit, manifesting uncontrollable laughter and others were infused with power to read their Bible more or pray more fervently.

I had already received much of the teaching necessary through audio cassettes, books and videos, before joining a signs and wonders Church. But the fine tuning had come from the teaching of the Signs and Wonders advocates. I could see this teaching was not just among the Word-Faith Ministers, much of it had now been accepted into the Charismatic and Pentecostal Movements themselves. This gave me the opportunity to expand my ministry and receive greater exposure. I had what many in the Church today are running after — real power, the power of the Holy Spirit, in my life.

I remember one of the most successful meetings I held. It provided me with convincing 'proof' of the presence of God's Holy Spirit in my life. People in the congregation responded directly to my pronouncements from the front, and the resultant signs and wonders were the strongest evidence validating that what I had been taught about phenomena was real. *I was now actually doing it!*

I ran around the room at full pelt, blowing on people. I had already noted where the most responsive people were sitting during the prolonged worship session. Their responses were astounding. Some were experiencing ecstasies for some time on the floor. Others shook energetically and praised God with mantra-like chanting. When the meeting was at a crescendo I remember experiencing the most intense exhilaration in the pit of my stomach. And whilst all this was going on, my mind was racing as my senses felt acutely aware of all that was happening.

I had become incredibly sensitive to the smallest details while under anointing and noticed the slightest gestures of the body language of others which I used well that night. This enabled me to pinpoint those who were being touched and focus on them during the 'manifesting ministry' time . On my way home that night I felt electrically-charged. I had received a wonderful gift offering (of money) and the Church was profoundly blessed and encouraged by my ministry. I now knew that my years of effort and sacrifice had paid off. God's calling on my life had truly begun in earnest. OR HAD IT?

Fiddler on the roof

In this classic story the Israeli actor Topol, who plays the leading role, delightfully portrays the plight of the Jewish nation. A nation which is eking out an existence while the whole world seems to be arrayed against it. They themselves make life more difficult by sustaining their own traditions. For the 'Fiddler', truth and reality seem at odds. This, in part, depicts the beginning of the struggle with my new found 'anointing'. I believe it also accurately depicts the struggle that many others are, even now, going through in their spiritual walk.

What do you do when Scripture and experience apparently contradict each other? How do you cope when your leaders reveal obvious and major theological flaws? (eg. when they tell you 'don't analyse' when Scripture says 'Test all things' 1 Thessalonians 5:21). This is when your Christian walk can become as precarious as a fiddler on the roof. When you discover that the great and marvellous Church, denomination or 'move of God' you are in, may well be full of the world, contradicting the Bible and developing its *own* tradition.

My situation was no exception. We preached prosperity, but always needed more money. We had all the gifts and anointing, but the weekly queues for deliverance never got any shorter. And although we had the power of the Holy Spirit, it only seemed to work on 'believers'.

Every time we had had a well-known, international speaker teaching at our Bible school, it was traditional to have him or her minister to us by laying his or her hands on us – to impart their anointing. I have had every Tom, Dick and Harry lay their hands on me, as did my fellow students. I had seen it done on videos and at crusades. It is, of course, fairly standard fare in the Signs & Wonders Movement. Although these days it can be someone blowing on you, throwing an item of clothing at you or even wagging his finger.

Anyway, this had begun to raise major concerns for me. The first was the effect I observed in my own life and in the lives of my fellow students. Please remember that all of us had been taught by, and prayed over by, the most anointed men and women of God that had traversed the planet! If anyone was going to save the world, it was us.

I attended the big crusades and ate, drank and slept the tapes and videos. Even so, there were still major problems, things that could not be reconciled. Preachers were teaching how to get and give the 'anointing'. Nevertheless, it was quite clear that, in truth, even their lives remained unchanged and that this was often reflected in their dealings with practical issues, like money.

One story which illustrates the many concerns I was having relates to the testimony of a 'faith' teacher called Norvel Hayes. Hayes tells how the Lord told him to raise an offering to buy Faith gurus Kenneth and Gloria Copeland their own home. Now I know we should help the homeless but just a few days later Kenneth and Gloria gave Norvel Hayes a lift to the airport in one of their two £32,000 Mercedes cars (this figure would be at least double today). *Norvel Hayes was being flown home in Kenneth's PRIVATE jet.* (see *Financial Dominion* by Norvel Hayes/Harrison House 1986) The point is they were hardly poor or homeless. The more I learned about the inner workings of the 'Faith' or 'prosperity preachers', the more their message and mission appeared to me to be actually at odds with the words of Jesus.

Many of the ministers from the Word Faith Movement/Signs & Wonders Movement demanded five figure sums even to come and minister in Britain. They often insisted on five star hotels, first class flights, frequently incurring costs of £30,000 + for four or five days of ministry in Britain. At this point I rationalised my concerns in the belief that at least many were being saved and healed – or so I thought.

But, on a practical level, nobody seemed to be prospering financially from all the "seed sowing" that was taking place except the Faith/Prosperity preachers themselves!! 'Have a need, sow a seed ' they teach, but I realised quickly that the unsaved were just as prosperous as Christians. The argument that it was the devil blessing the unsaved was becoming decidedly thin.

What I perceived is an example of "fruit machine theology". Every so often you would have a pay out that made your circumstances temporarily better and would keep you 'believing'. But the overall 'output' never matched the 'input'. For the most part the other students (many from Africa and abroad), worked very, very hard to make ends meet. But they were often unable to meet their Bible school fees and graduated in debt. My Church was about £200,000 in debt. It all just didn't add up! More and more charismatic/pentecostal Churches with the prosperity mentality are today in debt, some seriously.

One incident that really brought it home to me was when American Faith teacher Frederick K.C Price held a seminar in London at £25 per ticket. People were encouraged to "sow" £500 into his ministry whilst he sat on the stage wearing a suit and shoes I knew to be worth thousands of dollars. I had previously worked for a Paris designer company and I know £1,000 shoes when I see them.

And yet, everyday, hardworking people, mostly Afro/Carribeans, would shuffle down to the front of the Church meeting, with their plastic Woolworth's bags and C & A shoes, and hand over their hard earned money to receive God's blessing, to someone who would not come to England unless he was flown first class and was put up at a five-star hotel.

Another Faith teacher came to my Church during a convention and told us that *God had shown him* that morning (note the recurring theme: this was not my idea, but God's direct private revelation) that 91 blessings were contained in Psalm 91. He said they were available to everyone who would sow £91 by faith into *his* missionary work that day. I knew it was all wrong. A few days later whilst preaching at another venue in Brixton this same speaker had miraculously received the same revelation for his next audience to obtain the same blessings!

Jesus never taught or practised this sort of thing. Peter didn't have silver or gold at the Beautiful Gate, but the Holy Spirit was with him. But the Faith teachers were, I was beginning to see, even distorting Scriptures like these to show that the apostles were wealthy and not poor.

The ministries we should all be supporting are the ones that preach the true gospel, which helps orphans and widows, the homeless and the spiritually and materially hungry. Most of the ministers that came through our Church put on quite a show, with people 'slain in the spirit' and numerous reports of healings and other dramatic manifestations; the very things that I was now practising myself.

Virtually none of those who became 'converts' at our meetings, though, were ever seen again. At most of the big crusades the story was the same, and it still is. Thousands of converts are claimed every year *but virtually none of the converts can be found in a Church after the event.* This is especially true of Morris Cerullo's regular Mission to London. Although the Pentecostal Movement is the fastest growing denomination worldwide, two startling facts are widely unknown. First, in Western developed countries like America, N.Z, South Africa, Australia, and the U.K, its growth is largely by people drawn from other denominations. Second, where real Church growth is taking place through more biblical methods of evangelism, it is in places where the preaching of the gospel has been missing. The overall increase in attendance of evangelical Churches of all types is very small. It is in fact a fraction of the figures quoted by the big crusade organisers.

But I was witnessing more and more disturbing incidents which deepened my concerns about some ministries and even the great 'move of God' I believed I was in. I was at a Benny Hinn Crusade in Wembley when a man came on to the stage to testify of God's healing. Benny asked him what the Lord had done for him He testified God had healed his eyes, which, he said, had been crossed. Benny touched him on his forehead and he fell to the floor. "Oh, that's the power of the Holy Ghost", said Benny. The trouble was that I knew this individual had visited our Church several times trying to help escort some of the young ladies home! At first, he was Arabic, complete with traditional headgear, on another occasion he was "Jewish", complete with Kippur and side tassels. He definitely had some wires crossed somewhere. But on no occasion was he crossed-eyed! Benny Hinn could not, of course, be expected to know all this. But then why did the Holy Spirit touch him and knock him over? Surely the Holy Spirit knows when He is being lied to? He certainly knew when Ananias and Sapphira lied to Him and they paid the penalty. I was starting to wonder if this really was a new move of the Holy Spirit or an old move of another spirit.

More and more I began to see this could not be the anointing that the Bible taught. Another incident related to Morris Cerullo's personal bodyguard. Why any Christian speaker should need a bodyguard at all is beyond me, but, many of these 'anointed' leaders have them. Paul was constantly in danger, but chose to rely on his faith in God.

"Godly" is also not the word I would use to describe what was captured on video at one Cerrullo conference. It captured an apparent assault by Roger Artz, Cerullos' bodyguard, on a 15 year old girl in Canada. During the ministry time Artz can clearly be seen to push his way behind the girl and, by depressing the pressure point in her left shoulder, pull her to the ground giving the appearance that she was "slain in the Spirit". She was, in fact, the victim of a classic martial arts manoeuvre (see video: *Anointed Miracle Explosion* MCWE 1991). Some might argue Morris had no knowledge of this. But he cannot be excused for appearing on stage the following day (seen on the same video), addressing the crowd, saying he 'did not know' whether the same little girl was at the meeting or not – fully intending to subsequently relate her story. Why was it a sham? Because Cerullo's own ministry team had already treated the girl to new clothes, shoes, hair-do and had already interviewed her for television in the remote truck outside.

Other 'anointed' leaders such as Rodney Howard-Browne are also given to wild public assertions. At London's Olympia between December 1st and 4th 1995 he stated that a thousand souls per week were being saved at his crusades. (They certainly were not at the 1995 meetings!). I wonder if a thousand a year worldwide can be found in ANY Church one month after his meetings. The problem is, no one checks or is able to confirm these figures, they are simply claimed and consistently re-told.

The Holy Spirit, it seemed to me, was anointing some dubious spokesmen to perform His signs and wonders. I knew in my heart this could not be right. More and more terrible contradictions emerged. A woman in my Church died after "being told how to obtain her healing in the Lord". She was prayed for by the minister who did not question her "revelation" but administered the "laughing anointing" necessary for her healing. She fell to the floor laughing uncontrollably and was pronounced healed. Within the year she was dead. She died from the exact same sickness from which she had allegedly been cured. She was a good woman with a lovely Christian husband and family. *Was she misguided in her belief or misled by the leaders?*

I knew that God could not be behind much of what I was witnessing. It was also now becoming increasingly probable to me that neither was He behind the manifestations at my own meetings. In wanting more of God I had been deceived into wanting more "power" and in seeking first the kingdom of God I was really building a name for myself and a movement. Was it a movement of God's own Spirit? Was God in it at all? Were thousands really being saved, healed and delivered? Was it anointing or hype? Was it healing or heresy, revival or apostasy? I was becoming increasingly sure that what I was witnessing was spiritual deception.

BRAVEHEART

Through my own determination to go back to proper Bible study, especially through the original language texts, I steadily saw where my teaching had been decidedly unbiblical. God, I know now, defines *Himself*, His actions, His thoughts, His wisdom, His blessings, and promises to us by His Word – written down in the Bible. This much I now understood, through God's grace, with piercing clarity. Any teaching or supposed private revelation from any source outside Scripture, however spiritual in appearance, *must be tested and discounted, if it does not accord with God's Word.*

Coming to this understanding was crucial for my spiritual walk with Christ. I would also suggest it may be crucial for yours – if you do not wish to be misled. *God has made it clear that His Word and His Spirit never disagree!* I now know this to be an eternal truth. It transformed my understanding and set me free to experience the real joy of the Christian life.

In my first Church, I could now see, they had taught a faulty Christology. According to them Jesus was not one Person of the Godhead but God the Father, Son and Holy Spirit rolled into one. They went so far as to teach that the doctrine of the Trinity was 'a lie from hell'. They taught we are saved by grace – but not without water baptism. The Scriptures, of course, teach we are justified by faith alone! But, above all, they clearly did not understand the doctrine of the tri-unity (the Trinity) of the Godhead and much of their theological misunderstandings about the work of the Holy Spirit flowed from that.

I could now see there were similar problems with the heart of the theology of the Signs and Wonders Movement. Their understanding of the person of the Holy Spirit is almost pantheistic (equating God to a force). They had replaced an utterly Holy God, from whose presence sinners would actually recoil in fear, with a so-called 'tangible presence' of manifestations and blessings. Such an atmosphere, in reality, removes the need of Christ-centred gospel preaching through which the Holy Spirit brings conviction of personal sin, not 'impartations' of power. All faulty understandings of the Godhead eventually lead to 'another gospel'. To understand who God is and what He commands, we must return to orthodox methods of interpretation in studying Scripture.

Anything that is not consistent with the overall truth of the Bible must be rejected. For example we are walking along the road and we find a wallet stuffed with money, a few business cards, no I.D and no address. £120 of crisp notes are staring us in the face and we have a £110 gas bill to pay! It is a bill we cannot possibly meet and we have been praying for help. If we take it to the police station the chances are no one will claim it! We may be tempted to say it is God's provision. What do we do?

The commandments say "Thou shalt not steal". But we found it! The commandments say "thou shalt not covet anything that is thy neighbour's". But we do not know who it belongs to. We consider our options. But what if the person who lost £120 is about to have their gas disconnected for want of the money? They live in a damp and cramped apartment with a sick infant. They may have worked 20 hours overtime for weeks to save the money. If we knew all this, would we act differently? If the answer is YES then we have to admit we are adherents of "feelology" and not theology. The point is this, it doesn't matter whether the person who lost the £120 is rich or poor, sick or healthy, God's Word is very clear what course of action we should take. It is *not* negotiable.

I have learned that my theology, my understanding about God, comes only from Scripture — nowhere else. God Himself has already defined Himself and His actions. Certainly some parts are less clear to us than others, but God has given us a mind and an intellect to work all these things out – from His self-revelation in *His* Word. This is theology. 'Feelology' defines God's Word as "whatever 'feels good' must be from God"!

When I watch *Sleepless In Seattle* I experience emotions, I hug my wife, maybe I have a renewed sense of the importance of true love and family commitment, but none of this is based on TRUTH. My feelings as they are being experienced are a reality, but they are not a representation of God's biblical truth.

Emotions make good servants, but terrible masters. I had previously been uncritically judging by what I felt, saw and heard. In the absence of underlying principles (in my case biblical principles) I was deceived. Subjective arguments based on subjective experiences do not point to objective truth, even for born-again Christians. Our experiences, real or otherwise, are an insufficient measuring rod for biblical truth. Please do not make the same mistakes I made! If you are caught up in the 'experiential' merry-go-round, know that you can get off. If you do, I guarantee that your own personal relationship with God will begin to change for the better, almost overnight. I guarantee that spiritually you will see much more clearly than ever – if you test all things through 'God's spectacles', the Scriptures. Do not be deceived that it is the Spirit alone who leads – *it is not true*. The Word and Spirit *always* agree.

For me all of this brought into sharp focus issues and experiences connected with the Signs & Wonders Movement including: baptism in the Spirit, healing, tongues, slaying in the Spirit and many other manifestations.

Believing in Christ, first and foremost *engages the mind*. I now see that saving faith can only come with understanding, as Scripture makes abundantly clear. An experience *can* lead to the mind becoming engaged, but it should not, under any circumstances, circumvent it. To know salvation and confession, a person *must* first understand it. Only then can the will and the emotions play their part. To teach the following, therefore, is entirely unbiblical: "This is the beginning. I believe the day is soon approaching when the presence of God will fall on a whole congregation and every sinner in the house will get saved". Rodney Howard-Browne (*Rumours of Revival Study Guide*, Nelson Word UK 1995). To believe in Jesus requires the believer to know *who*

He is (ie: the Son of God) and what sin is; that repentance and Godly sorrow may follow, in accordance with the Scriptures.

Salvation comes by preaching *the message of the cross*, **not by signs and wonders**, or by wisdom! Belief is an established pattern of thinking that is a precursor to an action. Angelic visitations, visions and supernatural phenomena are not, and never have been, the methods for bringing salvation. In the NT, supernatural encounters either bring opportunity to preach, or confirm the gospel message *already being preached*. Even Saul of Tarsus heard Stephen preach the longest recorded gospel message in the entire NT just before his Damascus Road experience. If you are witnessing supernatural phenomena *where the gospel is not being preached*, as I had been: BEWARE!

In my early years I had confused "feelology" with theology. But now I know experience cannot dictate doctrine. We must let doctrine in Scripture be the sole arbiter of truth. I am aware that our bodies can produce an array of goose bumps, tingling sensations, shaking or emotions that are all too easy to equate with the presence of the Holy Spirit. But these are no different to the emotions and reactions we experience when we watch a film. However, in his latest book "Welcome Holy Spirit" (page 29) Benny Hinn says, "Instantly, His presence filled my room, *enveloping me in a heavenly warmth once again*. For the next eight hours my Bible was open as the Holy Spirit taught me *about Himself* from God's Word."

Jesus clearly said the Holy Spirit *would not* testify of Himself but would testify of Him – Jesus (John 15:26). Scripture thus totally invalidates the possibility of the Holy Spirit telling us to worship the Holy Spirit (except in the concept of the Trinity), have a love affair with Him, talk to Him or ask Him directly to speak to us. We are not told to pray to Him, invite Him in, pray Him down, lift Him up, blow Him out, or fan Him on people!

We are not called to say good morning Holy Spirit, welcome Holy Spirit or slap Him on handkerchiefs and mail Him? The Holy Spirit operates by God's will, not by man's. He is not grieved because your shoes are not shiny (Katherine Khulman on *God's Generals* Roberts Liardon video Vol. 7) nor does He want you to stand on the specific step of a flight of stairs – so He can speak to you (Kenneth Copeland – *South West Believers Convention* video 1993). This is spiritual elitism where people have "secret revelation". And by teaching these things I myself had been misleading others and getting them to put trust in me – and not directly in God.

Pentecost was a time when the Holy Spirit manifested a supernatural sign through those first believers, as they declared the wonderful works of God in several languages. When you speak in tongues do foreigners hear the gospel in their own language? Don't get confused here. When Paul said in 1 Corinthians 13:1 "Though I speak with the tongues of men and of angels, but have not love", he was not saying *he could speak* with human and angelic tongues, read 1 Corinthians 1:10, his emphasis is *love* not tongues. If I say to you: "If you jump up and down all day, I still won't lend you five pounds", I am not suggesting that you should jump up and down all day. It is to make it clear that you won't get the £5 no matter how long you jump up and down.

Paul also asks, "Do all speak with tongues"? (1Corinthians 12:30). 1 Corinthians 12:10 also clearly indicates that the manifestation of different kinds of tongues is given to one for many, *but not given to all*!

Is your speaking in tongues 'different kinds of tongues' or is it the usual '*shundai, shundai, kushanda, kushanda*' (ie gobble-de-gook) variety? This is not the biblical speaking in languages that could be understood by the hearers, neither is the gospel being declared to anyone. Most of it is gibberish, *a learned procedure* much as I was able to learn the procedures that are today passing for 'signs & wonders'.

All charismatics/pentecostals I know pray, as I did, in tongues when they want to and for as long as they want to – but the sounds are always the same. Basically, they can pray in 'tongues' when they want. But by doing so this overrides two fundamental principles in Scripture: that the Holy Spirit gives the manifestation *as He wills*, and that they are praying in the Spirit *because they do not know how to pray with intelligent language*. They know exactly how to pray with this kind of tongues, evidenced by the fact that they do it at will. This is also not evidence that people fail to speak in tongues today, as correctly defined in the Scriptures. But it is evidence that most speaking in tongues today is nonsense and can be done by anyone – as it is, of course, in many other faiths. More alarmingly, I myself began to encounter cases where 'tongues' had provided false evidence of salvation. I have come across examples of people who had learned to copy the phenomena of speaking in tongues. It later became clear (including to them) that they were not regenerate believers.

Tongues may be *a* sign of a regenerate believer, but it is not *the* sign. Believers are known by their love for one another and by the evidence of the fruit of the Spirit (Galatians 5:22) which is "Love, joy, peace, longsuffering, kindness, goodness, faithfulness, gentleness, self-control." *Not gifts!*

We are baptised in the Holy Spirit when we are saved. We should, thereafter, go on being filled with the Holy Spirit as believers. But it should be made clear – *there is no such thing as Spirit-filled and non-Spirit-filled Christians*. There are, however, plenty of Corinthian Christians!

The Holy Spirit is promised to all who are justified, as with Abraham, by putting trust in the Messiah (Galatians 4). He causes us to cry 'Abba, Father' – *not* 'More Lord' as signs and wonders exponents would have us believe. This is a delusion. There is no doubt that the 'laughing revival' known as the 'Toronto Blessing', the most visible recent expression of the Signs and Wonders Movement, is endorsed by scores of British Christian leaders. They include: David Pytches, Gerald Coates, Sandy Millar, Colin Dye, Ken Gott, Bryn Jones, R. T. Kendall, Terry Virgo, Clive Calver, Don Double, Dr. Patrick Dixon, and a host of others worldwide including: Rodney Howard-Browne, Kenneth Copeland, Benny Hinn, Ray McCauley, Rick Godwin, David (formerly Paul) Yonggi Cho, Morris Cerullo, Andrew Evans, Ian Bilby and Bill Subritsky. Does it have God's stamp right across it! Yes – but not in the way these leaders think it does. In 2 Thessalonians 2:10 – 11 God says He will send a delusion upon those *who do not love the truth*. To escape the delusion I had become ensnared with, I had to return to a biblical definition of Truth.

Since my own reformation I have personally written to dozens of Church leaders worldwide about unbiblical beliefs and practices connected with a faulty signs and wonders theology. ALL those I have written to refuse to discuss issues of doctrine *publicly*, as the apostles and early Church did. Most avoid answering any issues to do with Scripture. The reality appears to be that they do not love biblical truth and are leading countless thousands away from Bible-believing Christianity towards another gospel, another Jesus, and another Spirit!

Some of the teaching of our own leaders here in the UK is just as incredible as that relating to the American and world scene. The US scene is graphically chronicled in Hank Hanegraaff's excellent *Christianity In Crisis* (Baker Book House).

Well-known Charismatic Pastor Colin Dye from Kensington Temple is a good example. In his book 'Building a City Church' (Dovewell Communications 1993) he says "Churches will have the spiritual authority necessary to challenge the spiritual powers holding captive the populations of our cities" (Pages 43, 44). As an example, he cites the Ephesians: "They steamrolled through and pulled down mighty principalities and satanic strongholds" (page 45). This, once again, is mystical Christianity based on a faulty understanding of the Holy Spirit and pure 'feelology'. Undoubtedly, he was exercising the same spiritual 'authority' at the Wembley Arena with Paul "David" Yonggi Cho in 1995, when he encouraged the congregation to cast out 'a spirit of lawlessness and pray in a spirit of law-abiding (sic)' (*From the Heart with D. Yonggi Cho*. 1995 video – Dovewell Communications).

Apart from the fact that Dye totally misinterprets what 'pulling down strongholds' actually means (it means patterns of thinking and thoughts) there is NO example in Scripture of the apostles doing anything like it. They concentrated on preaching the gospel, which is the power of God unto salvation.

However, if we were to look closely at eastern religions we find exactly the same concept. It is the idea of dualism; light and dark, the good and bad side of the force in which we need the good to dispel the bad! POPPYCOCK, the only thing in the heavenlies are their brains. *Do not make the same mistake I did and follow them in their delusion.*

God is omnipotent—He does not need us to do anything to obtain victory other than to preach the gospel. And if this version of so-called 'spiritual warfare' works, why is it that W.H.Smith on the corner of the street where Kensington Temple (Colin Dye's Church) is situated still sells pornography from its top shelf? IF SPIRITUAL WARFARE CAN'T REACH THE END OF THE STREET, HOW WILL IT REALLY REACH THE HEAVENLIES? Somebody needs to tell the Emperor, he's wearing no clothes!

My reason for pointing this out, is that God will not work with, or through, error. I hope that as a brother in Christ, Colin Dye will change his mind about this nonsense and lead his congregation into biblical evangelism. And although no doubt very sincere, he is in fact revealing a distinct lack of *biblical* discernment, strongly evident from many of his comments, including this one from *Directions* magazine, April 1995, "We must not dare test the work of the Spirit!" One must already be predisposed as to what is or isn't the Holy Spirit, to follow this unbiblical teaching. The Scripture *commands us* to test ALL THINGS. This includes whether a work, an act, or a word is of the Holy Spirit or not. God Himself exhorts us to try Him, reason with Him and put Him to the test, so that we are certain we are following His Spirit. Doing this set me free.

Many other leaders are spreading this same delusion to seek for more of God. If anything, He probably wants more of us. Terry Virgo claims John (Pastor of the Toronto Airport Vineyard Church) and Carol Arnott have led the way in demonstrating an insatiable appetite for "more of God". Now "giving away" is the predominant theme. There is no attempt to claim ownership of this blessing. Arnott says, "My hope is that this book will serve TO INTENSIFY PEOPLE'S THIRST, expectation, and enjoyment of God's powerful presence in and through His Church." (*capitals mine-MH*: *Keep The Fire*, Marshall Pickering 1995). This totally unbiblical "thirsting for God" is central to the teaching of Arnott's book *Keep The Fire*. Among their many heretical statements they claim Jesus' body was bloodless on the cross before all our sin was placed on him and his body was contaminated. Carol Arnott even marries Jesus in a vision and becomes the bride of Christ! By seeking a sign, Carol Arnott has committed spiritual adultery by thirsting for feelings and manifestations. This leads away from the God of the Bible to the god of this world.

I now work in evangelism and Bible teaching. But I do not get up and pray for another 'feeling' or touch of something before I can carry on. If I gauge my ministry on experiential goose bumps and feelings, I would become an addict to sensations, not going out for the lost unless I have some kind of validating sensations.

I had come to know that the feelings and experiences of the Signs and Wonders Movement are not the Holy Spirit. So what is happening? Clearly something supernatural often appears to take place. There is nothing new in this. History shows such things are clearly the outworkings of dangerous shamanistic and hypnotic, mixed with strongly psychological, techniques as you will see later in this book. They are validated by poor biblical exegesis and a Christian name-tag. Those who are leaders in the movement dream of revival and mass evangelism that the Bible simply does not promise.

Whether leaders are conscious of it or not, they are promoting heresy through which God will not work. Whilst it is connected to evangelism, it is not true evangelism at all! Just listen to the words of Frederick K. C. Price (one of the many Word-Faith leaders I had been taught to follow) "Now this is a shocker, but God has to be given permission to work in this earth realm on behalf of man. Yes, you are in control! So if man has control, who no longer has it? God. When God gave Adam dominion, that meant God no longer had dominion, so God cannot do anything in this earth unless we let Him. And the way we let Him or give Him permission is through prayer" (*Christianity In Crisis* study Guide page 40).

Paul "David" Yonggi Cho is another, "You create the presence of Jesus with your mouth. If you speak about salvation, the saving Jesus appears, if you speak about divine healing, then you will have the healing Christ in your congregation, if you speak the miracle performing Jesus, then the presence of the miracle performing Jesus is released. He is bound by your lips and by your words. He is depending on you" (*The Fourth Dimension* – page 84). Is this a model for prayer or casting a spell?

Cho's meeting in London in 1995, was also endorsed among others by Roger Forster of Icthus, Gerald Coates of Pioneer, Lynn Green of

YWAM, HTB's Sandy Millar, and Kensington Temple's Colin Dye who were all at the same meeting. Colin Dye reflects Cho's dualistic (the equal battle between God and Satan being fought out on the earth) teaching, with this statement: "Now in the lower areas, we're going to pray against lawlessness and in the raised areas we're going to pray in law abiding (sic). So we're praying it out and praying the opposite in! Now are we together in this, are we united in the Holy Spirit?" (*From The Heart* video – Dovewell Communications 95).

Gerald Coates, one of the promoters of this event, was not in ignorance of the nature of Cho's teaching. It was pointed out to him, in written correspondence, beforehand. Yet he still endorsed the conference, featuring a man who teaches shamanistic and occultish visualisation technique as Christian doctrine.

Just like I was, many people are being deceived wholesale with this kind of "power" Christianity. The world is *not* held in balance by our lips, *God is absolutely sovereign*. Very subtle brainwashing techniques are being sown into people's minds. "Watch out for heresy hunters", they say, "they bring division". Rubbish! It is false doctrine that brings division! Don't worry, they say, if this *looks* like hypnotism, occult, shamanism, visualisation and metaphysics. The devil always has a counterfeit for the things of God, we are told. With this kind of subtle spiritual disarmament, the leaders, instead of warning the sheep against error, are inoculating the flock against truth! Over and over this technique is used.

R.T. Kendall says, "We're so conditioned for the occult and for those in showbusiness that have hypnotism that we assume if it comes into the Church, anything that smacks of that, ah! It's of the devil. They don't realise that the occult, or what people do in the way of hypnotism, is the counterfeit, and we've seen so much of the counterfeit, that we're not prepared to affirm when God does something, like He's been able to do for years, but we just haven't seen it, we're not prepared for it, so we say it can't be of God" (*Rumours of Revival* video NW 1995). And you have been inoculated against truth again! If it looks like it, tastes like it, sounds like it and feels like it, guess what? IT IS!

Many Christians believe deception is for the cults or some group that doesn't even believe in Jesus. But deception is clearly Satan's primary mode of attack against the Church. Paul says to the Galatians, "who has bewitched you?" to the Corinthians "don't be ignorant", to the Church at Laodicea "anoint your blind eyes". THESE WERE ALL BELIEVERS.

Our task is to separate the false from the true, the light from the dark. The so called signs and wonders I had witnessed and practised myself were and are nothing more than hype and the flesh, brought about by mindless worship and psychological crowd manipulating techniques. Most of what you see passing as 'anointing' and 'miracles' in Signs and Wonders meetings *can be learnt by anyone*.

Many of you reading these words may be devastated, as I was, after realising you have been duped by false teachers and false prophets, but do not give up. You are not the first and you won't be the last. Remember my story! It may be very painful but you will need to get out now before it is too late. And do not look back. You cannot remain in these Churches and not be influenced. Spend time with God and above all with His Word – read what it *actually says* for yourself.

One final thing. Prayer, for people coming out of the Signs and Wonders Movement deception, can be very difficult. I can remember finding prayer terribly difficult for a while. I had learned to gauge my spiritual walk and understanding on 'words from the Lord', and 'anointed revelation'. My first thought had been: 'What do I do now?'. It seemed like everything I had believed had turned out to be false. This is why the Bible calls it a 'great falling away' (2 Thessalonians 2). The Ethiopian Eunuch in Acts 8 made it with just God and a Bible and so can you! The Lord will lead you when you know His revealed word. Unfortunately, you may have already fallen prey to another spirit speaking to you. But, we have a more sure word of prophecy, the Word of the Living God, HE HAS ALREADY SPOKEN, you do not need "A Word" when you know THE WORD.

As I come to the end of my part in this book, my heart is heavy. The false doctrine of prosperity teaching all too often results in ruined lives. It causes broken marriages, depression and confusion borne of 'deliverance' ministry at the expense of Biblical teaching and discipleship. I know, I have seen it and been involved in it. It may be that as you read my story, you are aware of blatant contradictions in the teaching or lives of your leaders. Or, it may just be an inner sense or conviction that 'something is wrong'. You may be too scared to challenge the leaders for fear of being labelled divisive. You will no doubt be told you must "submit" to their leadership. They will try to suppress your fears in the name of authority or unity – but remember that thousands of believers have the same unanswered questions and concerns. Please remember, we are called to obey *God and His Word - not man.*

If you need help, it is available, as you will see at the end of the book. As the title of this chapter suggests, you will also need a 'brave heart'. But God will be with you and will empower you to do what is right. May God bless your journey.

Note

1 The Word-Faith Movement preaches a gospel of personal health and wealth (prosperity teaching) for all who through their 'faith force' can trigger material and supernatural responses to their personal desires . God's Sovereign Will is effectively overridden. This 'faith-force' effects eternal spiritual laws to which God himself is subject. The Faith teachers see the outworkings of these beliefs, ie. supernatural manifestations, as contemporary 'signs & wonders'.

Chapter 2

Tasting the fruit of the "Toronto Blessing"

Chris Hand

Time plays tricks on us all. Past events can blur into one and, without the aid of a diary, it becomes difficult to remember precisely when they happened. But every so often, an event takes place of a completely different order. We can remember exactly when it happened. Some people are able to recall precisely what they were doing the day President Kennedy was assassinated. They can remember where they were, what they were wearing, who they were with. The sense of shock, bewilderment and the shattering of normality remains indelibly etched on the memory.

A Day To Remember

The arrival in May 1994 of the 'Toronto Blessing' in a Church, where I was a Pastoral Assistant and part of the leadership team, did not achieve the headlines that the loss of a great national figure would merit. Yet the effect on me was similar. The spectacle of hundreds of friends being called forward to receive the 'Blessing' and falling over en masse; the jumbled heap of 200 bodies on the floor; hysterical laughter and people wriggling around, as if they were fish, is still fresh in my mind.

Some were convulsed as if an electric shock had passed through them while others stood statuesque, as if turned to stone. Some lay motionless on their backs with their arms outstretched as if attached to invisible helium balloons. Frivolous, contrived and superficial testimonies abounded – I can remember the sense of confusion, perplexity, shock and horror, as if it were yesterday.

It seemed unreal and a dream from which my wife and I would soon awaken. Surely it was not possible that people we loved and respected could have fallen for this? Surely the nonsensical biblical justifications being advanced would be seen through – wouldn't they? Or, at least, the absence of such ministry in the life of the Lord and the Apostles would be noticed? In any event, it seemed self-evident that our behaviour, including our conduct around the communion table with prone bodies scattered across the carpet, was profaning the holiness of the Lord and the dignity of His Church? Evangelical Church history and the serious atmosphere of revival had nothing remotely in common with this 'fun' revival? And how could Rodney Howard-Browne, the 'Holy Ghost bartender', conceivably be an instrument of the Lord? But then why could only a few of us see through it? Were we really right, while so many were wrong?

I tried to stay loyal to my Church and friends. I tried to be normal, look unruffled and carry on as usual. Perhaps it was not so dangerous as I first feared. Perhaps it would all go away soon. Ministerial colleagues and those that I looked up to did not seem to be too worried. There was even talk of conversions. Maybe God could be using this? Maybe I was the proud Pharisee? Even if my initial perceptions were right, perhaps I should stand by the Pastor I loved and the colleagues I had worked with, to help pick up the pieces and organise our public declaration of repentance and restitution when eventually the deception was exposed?

But, sadly, it was the 'Blessing' that stayed and it was I who had to go. The nightmare proved all too real and after a summer spent in a shocked state of mind, just like a rabbit caught in the glare of a car's headlights, it was time to part company.

The Parting Of The Ways

In truth, the realisation that all was not well in the Signs and Wonders world had been dawning on me for some time. There had been a steadily mounting case building up in my mind against many 'charismatic' teachings largely connected with the influence of the Signs and Wonders Movement. In the earlier days of my own experience there had seemed much that was good about being 'slain in the Spirit'. The availability of God's power to the Church had seemed like a wonderfully liberating experience. 'Holy laughter' was not invented with the 'Toronto Blessing' and, having seen it, even experienced it in years gone by, it seemed to have things in its favour.

Serious questions, however, remained. A number of features did not add up. The accounts in Acts did not indicate widespread 'signs and wonders' beyond the apostolic company. New Testament healings and works were vastly superior to those that I had witnessed. I was also compelled to admit that there was no great change in my own spiritual life stemming from my various experiences. 'Holy laughter', being 'slain in the Spirit', and supposed deliverance, had not produced greater holiness or effectiveness. This was before any account was taken of the false prophecies and the strange doctrines that many appeared to adopt in the wider and wilder 'charismatic' world.

It needs to be said that my former Church had *not* been involved with the Word-Faith or prosperity teaching of Morris Cerrullo or Kenneth Copeland. The Church would not have endorsed them in the normal way. Neither was it that we were experiencing tongues, prophecies and warm fuzzy feelings every morning, noon and night. Some pursued them enthusiastically but others were considerably more sceptical. Did the members of my former Church suddenly turn into crazed preachers of heresy, overturning the doctrine of the Trinity, the deity of Jesus Christ or the need to preach the cross? On the surface, the answer was again 'No'. The Church made much to the world of how the 'Toronto Blessing' enhanced orthodox doctrine.

But there was a deeper problem which this sad episode exposed. It is a problem that applies to the whole 'Signs and Wonders' Movement. As in the case of my former Church, its supposedly evangelical beliefs and creed were belied by its non-evangelical practice. We were evangelical by name – but, no longer, by nature. After reflection, prayer, and through the encouragement of some good friends outside the movement, I had to conclude that my previous involvement had been a mistake and that I needed to repent.

Fruit Assortment

To return to 'today', it is noticeable that the 'fruit' of the 'Toronto Blessing' continues to impress Christians. This includes some who would usually be alarmed by phenomena like 'slain in the Spirit'. So we need to ask 'What is the 'fruit' of the 'Blessing'?' What results has it achieved?

Since this phenomenon is essentially the latest expression of the Signs & Wonders Movement–a kind of compilation disc of the previous trends and emphases–our findings will apply across a wider spectrum of Christian life than simply the Toronto Blessing.

For convenience, the 'fruit' has been grouped together under five headings although they overlap considerably.

a) Improved spiritual life

Recipients of the 'Blessing' claim to have a greater desire for the Christian life and spiritual disciplines. Terry Virgo, leader of the 'New Frontiers' group of Restoration Churches, says:

"Regular Church prayer meetings are growing in numbers and in intensity. Also they are often going well beyond the normal time set aside....Spontaneous new prayer meetings are springing to life in many places as people gather to seek God. I have heard testimony of several having a new motivation to seek God... ...People want to be at God's house with God's people rather than spending time in other social preoccupations". [1]

In addition he records that: "Several have told me of new opportunities to witness, not only about the Lord Jesus in their personal lives but also of the presence of God in Church meetings". [2]

Laurence Barber, a senior pastor in a Canadian Church, commented upon the benefits he received from visiting the Airport Church in Toronto;

"As a result of my experiences at the Airport Vineyard, I have a renewed desire to share in Christ's concerns. God has led me to coordinate a local youth outreach.....He has given me a new desire to fellowship and work with other pastors and leaders in neighbouring Churches, whether or not we share denominational loyalties. And he has given me a new vision to reach the unchurched. Would anyone other than God have put these desires into my heart?" [3]

From the way this Pastor framed his question, he obviously expects the answer 'No'.

b) A sense of spiritual well-being

Others testify to having a greater awareness of divine realities. It is extremely common to hear people claim, for example, that they 'depend more on God', 'have more love for Jesus', or have greater 'intimacy' with Him. One woman reports:

"I feel different inside me and I feel beautiful. It is as if the Lord is blessing me and affirming me. I feel His pleasure in me and that makes me feel good". [4]

Taking a male example, one visitor to the Toronto Church remarked about his experience:

"When this work began in my heart after being prayed for, a new perception burst into my understanding: Jesus desired me! I couldn't believe it. I always knew He loved me. But I assumed that this was a heavenly sort of posture towards all creation. I never knew that He wanted me, longed for me, and desired me with real emotions". [5]

Experiences like these often lead to a greater relish for the Christian life.

c) Emotional and physical 'healing'

Other commonly recorded benefits might be classified as emotional release; dealing with past traumas and physical improvements in health.

Mark Stibbe in his book *Times of Refreshing*, quotes the testimony of one man who went to Toronto and whose experience began with the 'inner healing' of childhood memories. "The first person who prayed with me that evening enabled God to highlight old hurts that had built up in me, which had become a blockage to God's Holy Spirit. They prayed that God would take away the negative effect of words spoken to me when I was younger, particularly within my family". [6]

Often the areas 'highlighted' are very personal and very moving. Sometimes there are 'real' physical changes associated with the 'Blessing'. One such healing was recorded in *Anglicans for Renewal* Magazine where a vicar's wife suffering from ME, co-authoring with her husband, wrote; "She surrendered herself to God again, overwhelmed by a sense of his love – it became irrelevant whether she continued ill or well. Somebody prayed for healing anyway, and Anne felt a strong wind, and a tingling heat in her arms. She had been standing for much of this time, and was surprised to feel a lot better. As the meeting closed, she nervously walked out pushing the wheelchair in front of her".[7]

Her health continued to improve so that doctors were describing it as a "fantastic improvement" some time later (*Anglicans for Renewal* magazine Vol 62 1995:14). Testimonies in this category often overlap with the two given above. 'Inner Healing' and a sense of spiritual well-being often work hand-in-hand to produce a more disciplined spiritual life.

d) Repentance and behavioural change

Another aspect of the 'Blessing' is behavioural change. People reckon to become better people after spending time 'on the carpet'. Memories of things done or said flood back leading to repentance.

Another vicar's wife charted some of her experiences in the following manner; "All this time I was experiencing more and more strange 'phenomena'. Getting the giggles and laughing on more than one occasion, even at one o'clock in the morning. I also spent one night at home in bed sobbing and begging forgiveness for all the things I said (sic) and done that I thought were offensive".[8]

The Canadian pastor quoted earlier also experienced similar things as a preparation for his re-invigorated ministry. After falling to the floor, he observed; "A sense of peace followed my crying in which I knew that I was deeply known, forgiven, and loved in the presence of God. He also used this time to give me insight into my ongoing sin patterns, reassurance that deep emotional wounds were being healed, and reaffirmation of my direction for ministry".[9]

Others report the cure of drug addiction [10], the restoration of marriages [11] and various other positive behavioural changes.

e) Conversion and Church growth

The final category of fruit is that of Church growth either through the return of backsliders to the flock or through new conversions. These are perhaps the most powerful of the testimonies and evidences that are adduced. They are of themselves able to compel some acceptance, even among those that are disposed to be critical of some of the previous 'fruit' categories. Responding to a criticism that the 'Blessing' and, in particular,

Howard-Browne, are out to destroy the work of biblical evangelism and preaching, Dave Roberts (at the time Editor of *Alpha* Magazine) retorts, "... the facts are quite clear. Howard-Browne has seen thousands make a profession of faith since 1993. The Toronto Vineyard recorded between five and thirty conversions nightly. The Sunderland Christian Centre, who meet nightly, have seen high-profile local criminals and their families coming to Christ in the renewal meetings". [12]

Carolyn Allen, wife of Vineyard pastor Ron Allen, recorded in August 1994: "Last week we held tent meetings in the inner city. Not only did we see many healings, but over a hundred made first-time commitments to Jesus Christ. Fifty-five gang members gave up their caps and colours to follow Jesus Christ". [13]

This is a very brief resume of the 'fruit'. *It needs to be spelt out carefully that what is at issue are not 'facts'*. Some people doubtless are praying more or reading their Bibles more. Others are feeling better about themselves and have a deeper conviction that they love God and that God loves them. It should not be thought that people who claim to have turned away from some form of evil have not, in fact, experienced a behavioural change. Or that those who believe that they have been freed from a physical or emotional complaint have not in fact gained genuine relief, perhaps, even authenticated by the medical profession. I am not here suggesting people are wilfully and deliberately lying.

It has caused some people genuine perplexity and incomprehension that anyone should take issue with these 'plain facts'. Even the more half-hearted 'Toronto' supporters who have been unable to overlook the weakness of the biblical case for the 'Blessing' have cheered themselves up by pointing to the 'changed lives' and Church growth that have followed in the wake of the 'Blessing'. Those who have been unhappy with the manifestations and the origins of the movement have found, they believe, some 'good fruit' and consequently dubbed it a 'mixed blessing' to cope with the paradox of seeming good arising from doctrinal error. Indeed it has looked like the height of folly and an act of intellectual suicide to question the 'fruit'. Would the devil make people pray and read their Bibles more? Would evil beings really want to grant emotional benefits which people then attribute to God? Above all, would it be in the interest of the enemy of men's souls to see people 'led to Christ', and for Churches to grow?

And yet, this is the heart of the problem, for the answer to all these questions, under certain conditions, is actually 'Yes'. None of the testimonies detailed above are immune from investigation. Despite their appearance, each of the types of fruit is not self-evidently right or authenticated. There are deeper issues involved. Claims and testimonies, albeit well-meant, cannot be taken at face value. We have a duty to investigate further.

To help prepare the way for such an appraisal, there is a concept which can help peel the 'fruit' and to this we now briefly turn.

Paradigms Lost....

The concept of a 'paradigm shift' in our Christian thinking was introduced into the evangelical Church through the teachings of John Wimber [14]. A 'paradigm', quite simply, is the way we look at things. Central to Wimber's teaching is that the 'Western' mind-set has 'explained away' the supernatural and made everything subject to reason. His belief is that a 'paradigm shift' is needed to open people up to the existence of supernatural power. He is right that we presently need a 'paradigm shift', a change in how we look at things. He is desperately wrong in the direction he wishes that shift to be made.

It is a fact apparently lost on Wimber that an enormous 'paradigm shift' has already taken place in evangelicalism and has been quickly gathering pace in recent years. It is a shift that has only been observed by a comparative minority in the evangelical community, despite the fact that it has already led to fundamental changes. To sum it up, *while evangelical language has remained constant, evangelical practice has altered radically*. As I found out belatedly, the Church I thought was evangelical turned out not to be. It had orthodox beliefs on the Trinity and the deity of Christ, on the need for preaching and to 'reach the lost'. Yet its practice and thinking were thoroughly un-evangelical.

This is vitally important for any understanding of the 'fruit'. Although there are evangelical procedures to examine spiritual results, the 'paradigm shift' in thinking has, in fact, caused true spiritual examination to fall into disuse. For example, it is obvious that to evaluate anything properly we need to know what we are looking for. There is no point taking a car to be checked by someone who knows nothing about engineering, mechanics and car maintenance. We need someone with a detailed knowledge of how the brakes and clutch work, or how to test the electrical circuits, rather than someone who does a quick assessment based upon what the car looks like from the outside. Paintwork may be in pristine condition and the chrome trim spotless, but if nobody gets 'under the bonnet' to look for defects, we are none the wiser as to how roadworthy the vehicle actually is.

Procedures for evaluating spiritual life and progress have sadly reached a point in many nominally evangelical Churches where they are nothing better than a quick spot check of the paintwork. The science of thorough spiritual examination (discernment) has all but been lost. Most ironic of all, though, it is among those claiming to be 'filled with the Spirit' that this decline is most pronounced. Many simply do not know how to examine and diagnose spiritual experiences. They do not think to get 'under the bonnet' to look more closely. Even if people do get round to asking questions, they are not sure what questions they should be asking or how satisfied they should be with the replies they are receiving. The 'paradigm shift' has happened by stealth and left much of the Church utterly unskilled in 'spiritual mechanics'. Put simply, many Churches have lost their evangelical mind.

Peeling The Fruit

This 'paradigm shift' away from evaluation and investigation is apparent in the way that the 'bad fruit' or the 'none fruit' of the 'Blessing' has been largely ignored. Much 'fruit' simply does not fulfil the most basic of evangelical expectations.

Some Churches, for example, give no indication of greater spiritual discipline, prayer or Bible reading. While testimonies are rushed into print or people are hurried on to the platform to testify to their latest emotional healings, many have gained nothing from the experience. It simply did nothing for them. Or perhaps it gave them a sense of 'peace' but nothing else. Anything to show that either the individual or the corporate life of the Church had changed, was absent. Yet to say that the Spirit came down and did 'nothing' is in evangelical terms an impossibility. Something has gone wrong somewhere.

In my former Church it was often a cause of acute embarrassment for me to hear testimonies that could offer no evidence of lasting change. The principal sum of the testimony was often to the effect that: 'Something happened to me, but I'm not sure what'. The euphemism that the 'Lord is doing a deep work in me' became the substitute for the more honest 'I haven't got a clue why I laughed or started to cry'. People would cast around for something more to say, but would often have to settle for saying that they 'loved Jesus more' in the absence of anything more substantial to report.

In many situations there has been no Church growth to report. It has not brought unbelievers streaming in through the doors, for all the wild claims we hear. When some have ventured in they have not been struck by the awfulness of their sins or of the awesomeness of God's holiness. Some have found the spectacle 'interesting' or been made curious but it has not typically brought a sense of the need for sins to be forgiven. Indeed in some cases there has actually been Church decline. Fellowships have been riven asunder with the flock scattered to the four winds. Over-bearing pastors and leaders have threatened, cajoled, stonewalled and manipulated to get the 'Blessing' into Churches. Confused believers with serious biblical reasons for their concerns have been shown the door and some remarkable extremes of stupid and arrogant leadership are now a matter of historical record. Many leaders have shown a reluctance to discuss the issues on biblical grounds or have advanced a shambolic caricature of biblical exegesis to justify the antics of the 'Toronto Blessing'. Again, something has gone wrong somewhere. Bland assertions of good *and lasting* fruit are simply untrue.

Returning, once again, to my former Church, I did see a number of non-believers come through the doors but they went back through them in exactly the same state. There was no evidence of conversion although some claimed to 'love Jesus' or to have experienced 'peace'. Published statistics of conversions and returning backsliders bore no relationship to the actual reality. Following up some of these people revealed their confused state of mind and yielded very unsatisfactory results. Attendance at some Church prayer meetings *actually declined*. One reason being that people were too tired for work after staying late at the meeting the night before. Other prayer meetings degenerated into 'receiving meetings' when the 'Blessing' was dispensed to the thirsty.

Examples of emotionally vulnerable people suffering great harm through the 'Blessing' have surfaced with grim regularity, some being personally known to me. People have heard voices, been plagued with blasphemous thoughts and become severely depressed through involvement in the 'Blessing'. Even the prospect of the 'Blessing' being foisted upon them has driven a few into confusion and spiritual depression. Others have candidly admitted an addiction to the 'Blessing' and spoken of an obsession that interfered with the performance of work and domestic responsibilities. There have been a few isolated reports of people being unable to suppress the desire to roar at work or in the supermarket queue.

Such 'bad' experiences and 'non-event' experiences are more common than admirers of the 'Blessing' are willing to concede. This betrays an anomaly. Practitioners sincerely believe they are imparting the Holy Spirit. People are taught and encouraged to switch off their minds to receive Him. Yet identical mind-emptying processes lead one to have a 'good' experience but lead another to have a 'bad' or 'non-event' experience. For some it is like rushing to the telephone only to find it was a wrong number or a nuisance caller. How is this to be explained? Is it a problem at the recipients' end as the supporters of the 'Blessing' are compelled to claim? A 'blockage', a hidden sin perhaps? Is it that people have a 'fear of emotions' or a 'fear of deception' that prevents them 'receiving'? [15] Or might the answer not be a lot simpler. Perhaps it is not the Holy Spirit in the first place? The anomaly of 'bad' and 'non-event' experiences is explained not by a deficiency in the 'recipient' but by a deficiency in the 'power' that is at work. In plain English, the Holy Spirit cannot produce 'bad fruit' but other darker forces can.

Trivial Pursuits

From personal experience I know there is also gross over-reporting of the benefits. Every conceivable benefit of the most trivial kind is attributed to the 'Blessing'. Vague coincidences and rambling 'blessed thoughts' are traced back to time spent on the floor in a trance-like state. Utterly banal, ridiculous and incoherent testimonies are trumpeted abroad without any quality control being exercised. The 'best' testimonies which get into print are the tip of a huge iceberg of inconsequential, nonsensical and contrived testimonies which need only the most elementary grasp of Scriptural reasoning to be dismissed. All this is to be found simply by 'lifting the bonnet' and daring to have a look. Whole 'fleets' of these gleaming testimonies turn out to be engine-less.

Again, in my previous Church there were supposed 'sightings' of the Lord pouring out water which people 'saw' while lying on the carpet. Others were running through cornfields with Him while others saw His 'pearly white teeth'. One 'saw' the Lord with the imprint of the nails now mysteriously gone from His hands. Others reckoned to hear angels singing or received prophecies about the great revival that was coming. The similarity of many of the claimed visions or revelations was striking and it is difficult in words to portray the banality and triviality that characterised them.

Simple evaluation throws up some more anomalies. For example, people claiming to be vastly different turn out to be exactly the same. Without meaning to be unkind, the people I worked with at my former Church remained about the same for all the fullness of the Spirit that they were supposed to have. Some had spent hours doing 'carpet time' without any evidence to show for it.

Away from the meetings, topics of conversation amongst 'recipients' are the same as usual, people's moods and mannerisms following predictable courses. Some folk, like roads which are constantly being dug-up and re-instated for repair work, are always needing further treatment 'on the carpet'. Minor and insignificant happenings are blown-up out of all proportion while people lie semi-conscious on the floor. New 'problems' are exposed requiring further treatment and, depending on the ethos of the Church, repentance is advised, demons are cast out, visualisation practices (a technique borrowed from the occultish Shamans) are undertaken or 'blockages' dealt with through 'deeper' ministry.

People are simply not listening to themselves. Many simply do not realise that much of what they say is self-centred, glib and trivial.

No Questions Asked

One very worrying tendency is the way that posing questions is deliberately short-circuited. This is never a sign of 'good fruit'. Critics have been labelled as 'unbelieving', 'blasphemers against the Spirit' or 'anti-charismatic'. By rubbishing opponents of the 'Blessing' in this fashion, it has let some off the hook from having to interact seriously with their critics. Others chide critics for speaking out and going into print rather than bringing their disputes to be settled in private. This ingenious reasoning overlooks the fact that they themselves are aggressively publicising their meetings, publishing numerous books and issuing pronouncements and teachings from pulpits. When they have been spoken with in private (which many of them have!) there is no evidence of substantial change in outlook or practice as a result.

The warning 'Take heed that you be not deceived' (Luke 21:8), a solemn charge given by the Lord to His own disciples, is also brushed aside as today's believers are promised 'diplomatic immunity' from deception and assured that it could never happen to them. This teaching has been repeated in my own hearing and is by no means uncommon. Such views are held despite the ample material in Scripture on false prophets and false teachers arising to deceive the Church (for example Deuteronomy 13:1-5; Jeremiah 23:9-40; Ezekiel 13; Matthew 24:11, 23-26; Jude 4-19). While claiming to be alive to the possibilities of the evil one and the flesh at work in 'Toronto' meetings, Sandy Millar, one of the most prominent leaders of the 'Toronto' movement in the UK, is not able to provide any credible guidance. [16] The technique to impart the 'Blessing' is applied uniformly and indiscriminately, people being coaxed down the same mind-emptying path, encouraged in effect to play spiritual Russian roulette in the hope that that they are not receiving a demonic or fleshly experience.

As for some of the 'personal' and 'emotional' blessings, a most cursory exploration of Scripture points to their inadmissibility. 'Feel-good' testimonies and self-preoccupied 'inner healings' are absent from the pages of the Bible. In fact Scripture insists on the need to look beyond self to things above, to be 'other-worldly' rather than 'this-worldly' (Colossians 3:1-4). Self-centred experiences are not the hallmark of the Holy Spirit, however much good the person may feel they have derived from them. Even testimonies of the 'spiritual well-being' variety often collapse into nothing more than issues of 'self-esteem' dressed up in Christian clothes. Such 'blessings' fall at the first hurdle of biblical investigation since they are nowhere marked out as signs of spiritual growth and maturity.

In other words, many testimonies and claims should be screened and eliminated by asking one simple and evangelical question – *is it in the Bible*? It is a simple test which is within the reach of all evangelicals. Sadly the 'paradigm shift' has made it an unfashionable one to pose. Yet from personal experience and familiarity with the burgeoning pro-'Toronto' literature, this simple test sweeps away the majority of recorded 'blessings'. The testimonies may be very moving, but if Scripture has nothing to say about them, then neither should we.

Getting To The Core

The crux of the matter is the place of Scripture in the interpretation of experience. In essence it is quite a simple issue that has been obscured over the years through neglect. Christian experience, if it is to be such, must by definition be produced by the Holy Spirit. It is as simple as that. Spiritual experience that is not produced through the agency of the Holy Spirit is not a genuine spiritual experience – *irrespective of how beneficial, helpful or impressive are its results.*

"Every good tree bears good fruit, but a bad tree bears bad fruit. A good tree cannot bear bad fruit, nor can a bad tree bear good fruit". (Matthew 7:17-18). Whatever fruit grows out of a non-spiritual experience is *ipso facto* not genuine. It is the result of other forces and sooner or later *will* be exposed as such.

A key text to understand this is the description of the new birth. Its mode of impartation gives vital lessons.

"That which is born of flesh is flesh, and that which is born of the Spirit is spirit. Do not marvel that I said to you "You must be born again." The wind blows where it wishes, and you hear the sound of it, but cannot tell where it comes from and where it goes. So is everyone who is born of the Spirit".(John 3:6-8)

Spiritual life can only be initiated by the gracious work of the Holy Spirit and comes from outside. Man is spiritually dead (Ephesians 2:1-3) until the new birth. Regeneration, repentance, faith and conversion, while they crucially involve and engage man's faculties, proceed from God. They do not come from within man. Experiences which have their source within the soul, as a result of man's efforts, are not spiritual. They are a work of the flesh no matter how spiritual sounding or impressive their achievements.

Later in John's gospel, the Lord again remarks,

"It is the Spirit who gives life; the flesh profits nothing. The words I speak to you are spirit, and they are life." (John 6:63)

The work of the new birth comes from outside, *through the preaching of the Word which enlightens the mind*. It quickens the conscience and stirs the emotions with the spiritual truth it imparts. It acts upon the mind to impress upon it the lost state of one's soul, the utter depravity of man before God, the certainty of judgment and the glorious work of Christ in dying for sinners. It *may* be attended with great emotions (manifestations) or determination of will, but these will be a response to the revelation of objective truth. Critically it is a work that takes place in the waking and mindful state only. Indeed the alarm and heart-searching that result is rightly described as an 'awakening'. The mind and soul are never more exercised than when conversion is taking place.

The same principle applies to sanctification. It is done with one's eyes open. It is not carried out in a trance or through a bout of uncontrolled laughter. It is effected through the Word of God by the Spirit and leads to spiritual growth (2 Corinthians 3:17-18). Through adherence to revealed biblical truth it is possible to 'walk in the Spirit' (Galatians 5:25) which is indicative of growing Christlikeness. A life of faith and obedience marked by prayer and a deliberate application of truth produces the values, priorities, spiritual understanding and discernment that are the hallmarks of spiritual growth and maturity. In other words obedience has spiritual results and instils growing Christmindedness (1 Corinthians 2:16). It is not achieved by emptying one's mind or losing self-control, against which we are continually warned by the New Testament writers.

Applying The Test

How then does the remaining fruit of the 'Toronto Blessing' fare? Most of it is immediately ruled out of court. The techniques and ambient culture of the meetings ensure this conclusion. By using loud music, by calling forward previous recipients of the 'Blessing' and praying for them again in public, and by encouraging people not to use their minds but to 'receive/yield/drink', evangelical practice is aping the methods of hypnotists. The induction of 'altered states of consciousness' and the use of touch on strategic parts of the body to induce experiences are man-made forms of worship. They by-pass the rational faculty and produce a state of mind that is outside the scope of God's agency. Counsel 'to experience it first, analyze it later' is unknown in Scripture and therefore forbidden as a way to arrive at the new birth or to communicate revelation, bring about spiritual growth or impart giftedness in God's service.

This simple fact explains why these practices are not to be found in Scripture. The Lord Jesus never used them, neither did the apostles, neither any of the prophets of the Old Testament. They are not how the Lord reveals Himself or requires people to worship Him. This in turn explains why supporters have advanced such a weak and spurious biblical case. In the absence of biblical credentials they are quite simply having to manufacture a case of their own.

Even the seemingly unassailable claims of Church growth, conversion and greater spiritual discipline are exposed as deficient once the method of God's working is clearly seen. Most claims are explicitly disallowed through the words of the recipients themselves admitting that the benefits were obtained while in a self-induced 'altered state of consciousness'. These *automatically* fall outside the scope of the work of the Holy Spirit. Such experiences may well generate excitement that translate into missionary zeal or a greater relish for Church meetings, preaching, Bible Study and prayer. But the foundations are faulty. The zeal is built upon a false premise. How often it is heard that accelerated spiritual progress followed a manifestation as trivial as 'falling over'. Or a twitch supplied the necessary evidence that the person was loved by the Lord. Or roaring like a lion sent them off as missionaries. False conclusions are being drawn from wrong premises. People feel closer to God but really they are not. People think they are serving God but the truth is they are not. Ironically, the best evidence that a person has been 'blessed' is when they realise that the 'Toronto Blessing' and the Signs & Wonders Movement are deceptions. Until then, there is no ground for expecting that the person's desire for Bible reading or prayer will lead to any spiritual growth or make the person a fit instrument in His service.

On a very serious note, it is disturbing to hear of those who believe they have been converted through an experience, or who have been 'led to the Lord' after having undergone a manifestation. It is irresponsible pastoral counsel to assure such 'converts' that they have been saved on the basis of an experience such as the 'Toronto Blessing'. As has been seen, the Holy Spirit's work is conducted upon a person's soul with their 'eyes open' rather than in an 'altered state of consciousness', taught or induced with the help of others. This is not biblical evangelism and will not produce biblical conversions. What kind of gospel or Jesus are they being converted to?

Neither is conducting evangelism in the environment of such meetings likely to yield good fruit either. While some meetings are not devoid of gospel reasoning, when used in tandem with the 'visual aid' of the 'Blessing' in its various manifestations, the gospel message is virtually emptied of its power. Examples have come to light of 'evangelistic' services conducted without the preaching of the Word in the naive hope that the sight of a room of people 'manifesting' would produce conversions. Such expectations in themselves expose the spurious nature of the 'Blessing'. Peter preached the gospel on the Day of Pentecost (Acts 2:14-41) and so did the apostles when they were filled with the Spirit afresh a little later in the Acts narrative (Acts 4:31). The preaching of the word of God remained paramount whether signs and wonders were present or not. Evangelism conducted without preaching the gospel is not evangelism at all.

Even where space is given for some semblance of preaching, Church leaders are still keen to use the visual aid of signs and wonders like the Toronto Blessing. People who have been previously 'blessed' give accounts of their experience and then receive prayer to be 'blessed' so that their subsequent manifestations are visible and audible to the whole meeting. Two or three people may be prayed for in this fashion, the intention being to make the gospel account more 'credible' through a supposed demonstration of God's power through alleged signs and wonders. All this achieves, however, is confusion. Desire for the power on offer can supplant the hearing of the Word. Becoming a Christian is confused with 'receiving the Blessing', the gospel being interpreted in the light of people shaking, falling over, laughing and having visions. Since so many of the testimonies given by people at these meetings are utterly incoherent or centred upon building up self-esteem, it presents a grievously misleading picture of true conversion, mortification of the flesh and Christian discipleship. Coupled with the use of loud music and rhythms capable of producing 'altered states of consciousness', it can be appreciated that these meetings are not a safe environment for the conduct of evangelism.

It is worth pointing out here that the same observations apply when looking at the results of the *Alpha Course* promoted by Holy Trinity Brompton, West London, one of the chief UK sponsors of the 'Blessing'. The Holy Spirit Weekend, an integral part of the course, engenders similar experiences and courts the risk of producing spurious conversions. The fact that so many Churches involved in the 'Toronto Blessing' are conducting their evangelism through the mechanism of the *Alpha Course*, is not a cause for encouragement but for concern. Much of the missionary zeal forged out of the white hot heat of Toronto is directed towards persuading people to attend such courses or meetings where the 'Blessing' will be in evidence. Some of the reports that emerge from these and similar evangelistic endeavours highlight again the unsatisfactory testimonies of the 'converts'. Self-esteem, 'finding a purpose in life' and the resolution of personal trauma loom large, and it is difficult to detect repentance, fear of judgment, or absolute dependence on Christ for salvation. [17]

Making repentance and faith become works that come from 'within', especially if induced by an 'altered state of consciousness', rides roughshod over all the observations made earlier about the new birth and sanctification. Mistaken ideas about conversion, if taken and disseminated abroad, are not portents of future 'Blessing' or healthy Church growth. Cults, in general, do more 'evangelism/proselytizing' and display greater zeal than evangelicals but are far from presenting a rounded or accurate gospel.

None of this should in fact surprise us. This is not an unnecessarily hard approach to take. It is permitted by Scripture. The Lord Himself rebuked hypocrites who prayed (Matthew 6:5), castigated diligent but fruitless study of the Scriptures (John 5:39-40), bemoaned the making of false converts (Matthew 23:15) and dismissed behavioural change divorced from true spiritual change (Matthew 23:28). Many were doubtless very sincere in the pursuit of their religious devotions and were able to furnish evidence of progress as time went on. Yet when subjected to closer scrutiny they were found to be wanting. In the Lord's solemn words, 'Every plant which my heavenly Father has not planted will be uprooted' (Matthew 15:13). The implications of this are devastating. We ignore the Lord's prescribed methods and Scripture's teachings at our peril. None of the 'fruit' is immune to challenge and not to evaluate it more rigorously would be to abdicate responsibility.

Paradigms Regained

The 'paradigm shift' in evangelicalism has left its mark. It is now unfashionable to ask questions, to be critical of the source of spiritual experience, to doubt religious zeal or to believe that the professing Church can be deceived. In others words, to be evangelical no longer means that one has to accept the authority of Scripture. It is a desperate situation and needs urgent remedy.

Most important, on the subject of 'fruit', the 'paradigm shift' has left many Churches without the necessary equipment or skills to practise spiritual discernment. Like the untutored car mechanics referred to earlier, people are impressed with appearances and do not know how to check for the 'roadworthiness' of spiritual experiences. Few are willing to 'get under the bonnet' and even fewer know what they are looking for when they do. In some cases it is a sad admission that years of Bible teaching, Bible Weeks, ministry courses and charismatic 'life in the spirit' have proved to be utterly useless when a time of real and critical testing has arisen. A generation of professing evangelical believers has arisen, robbed of spiritual discernment and incapable of reasoning from Scripture. It is a tragic situation.

It is not the flock but the Christian leaders who have been largely responsible for this 'paradigm shift' away from Scripture. The 'Toronto Blessing' has cruelly exposed the superficiality of perception and evaluation among many, often untrained, leaders. Questionable practices and their 'fruitful' effects are accepted as long as they cheer people up, lead to greater numbers in Church and create a superficial veneer of moral behaviour. While such views prevail, it will simply prove impossible for people to see the real 'fruit' of 'The Blessing'. It will continue to impress, deceive and in turn provide fertile soil for the incubation of further deceptions and fresh mischief for the Church.

Yet the answer to the problem lies within the reach of the evangelical Church. A better 'paradigm' can be regained through repentance and turning back to the authority of the Scriptures. This is not just a call to daily Bible reading or memorising Scripture passages, valuable though these things are. It needs more. It is a call for a biblical mind.

The crying need is for the truth of the spiritual understanding of Scripture. Evangelical principles of interpretation and application have to be sought, and to accomplish this will need God's help. It is, for instance, a foolish misunderstanding to regard the study and application of Scripture as purely an intellectual exercise. Scripture can only be understood and comprehended with the aid of the Holy Spirit. The 'great divorce' between the Word and the Spirit, which some have suggested exists, is a fiction. It betrays a fundamental misapprehension about the function of Scripture as well as an inadequate view of preaching and conversion. The preached word represents the appointed means for the saving of men and women's souls. It is not merely the presentation of words which need the help of imitation 'signs and wonders' to give it a boost: it is itself the power of God for salvation

(Romans 1:16; 10:14-15) and has spiritual power which is beyond the simple communication of a series of theological propositions (John 6:63). Neither is it the intellectual assent to some received information. It is so much more. The 'spiritual' nature of Scripture and preaching needs to be urgently recovered, otherwise the future of hermeneutics, biblical evangelism, preaching and pastoral theology is bleak.

Recovery of a biblical mind is vital for the 'cure and care of souls'. Pastoral leadership has been weighed and found wanting. Nowhere has this been more apparent than in the capitulation of people who should know better before the altar of the fruit of the Signs & Wonders ministries. Too many people have been impressed with too little. To rectify this needs a ruthless task of examining assumptions and practices to see whether they are biblical. I began this chapter with my own story. Reformation has been the pressing need for my own life. It has been a humbling experience for me to admit my own wrong and lack of discernment in succumbing to the peer pressure involved in accepting the Signs & Wonders Movement at face value. But repentance has proved to be liberating. The sense of coming home through embracing Reformed Evangelical doctrine about the Church, about Scripture, its authority and proper use, leaves me still with a sense of profound gratitude to the Lord for His grace and mercy. The wisdom of the writers of a different generation who had learned to discern between counterfeit and genuine spiritual experience speaks volumes today in the face of confusion and widespread delusion and deception. Freed from the need to give credibility to the banal, the ridiculous, the plain wrong, and no longer required to pay lip service to the false gods of psychotherapy, the Church Growth Movement and other emasculated forms of evangelism, have opened up new realms of understanding previously only dimly perceived or known by rumour.

Sadly, my life and ministry is not the only one that needs such treatment. Reformation is required across large swathes of the nominally evangelical Church. Leadership, Churchmanship and discipleship in general have to grow wiser and much more biblically astute. Gullibility and credulity are luxuries that can no longer be afforded or tolerated. Questions have to be asked and the 'sufficiency of fruit' challenged according to Scriptural reasoning and spiritual insights. The people of God need to be better taught to be more discerning both about the state of their own souls and about the state of others.

All of these are tasks to be relished. No new teachings or revelations are needed as the Reformers and Puritans have been this way before. Our generation is privileged above any other in the opportunity it has to learn from their insights. Many Churches need to recognise that they have been sold a pale imitation of evangelicalism. Their practice no longer matches up to their evangelical creed. A quiet, subtle but wholesale 'paradigm shift' has been taking place and we need to return to the ancient paths.

This is a very exciting prospect, because such a reformation would meet the needs of the hour. Western society is in disarray and requires strong gospel preaching. A gospel undiluted by cheap imitations. A reformed Church would be a powerful instrument in the hands of Almighty God. It is a goal that is worth praying for and working towards, with all the strength that God gives us.

Notes

1 'Frontline' Magazine September 1994 p10

2 'Frontline' Magazine September 1994 p10

3 'Christianity Today' 11 September 1995 p26

4 In Dixon, 'Signs of Revival' 1994 p74, Kingsway, Eastbourne.

5 In Chevreau, 'Catch the Fire' 1994 p194, Marshall Pickering, London.

6 In Stibbe 'Times of Refreshing' 1995 p137, Marshall Pickering, London.

7 'Anglicans for Renewal Magazine' vol 62 1995 p13.

8 'Anglicans for Renewal Magazine' vol 62 1995 p16.

9 Laurence Barber in 'Christianity Today' 11 September 1995 p26.

10 'Good Fruit' 1995 Queens Road Church, Wimbledon, London.

11 Ken and Lois Gott in 'Weeds and Thorns uprooted in God's Garden' **'Renewal' Magazine,** February 1996 p44.

12 Dave Roberts 'Truth is the Casualty' in **ALPHA Magazine** February 1996 p6.

13 In **Chevreau,** ibid p157.

14 For example, **John Wimber** 'Power Evangelism' pp 74-96, Hodder, London.

15 See Rob Warner **'Prepare for Revival'** pp136-144, Hodder, London, for a typical list of reasons given by supporters why some receive so little.
16 Sandy Millar in 'We ask the Holy Spirit to come – and He does' **'Renewal' Magazine,** January 1996 p14.
17 See, for example, **'How Samantha Fox was touched by the Spirit'** in **The Baptist Times** 1 September 1994 p7.

Suggestibility, hysteria and hypnosis

Philip Foster

Human beings are suggestible. It does not matter who you are, your level of intelligence or your education: we are suggestible. Take a very simple example, the yawn. In a room full of people someone yawns, and before long so does nearly everyone else! Or someone who is experiencing a strong emotion joins a group. It has an immediate effect on everyone present. This is quite natural, even normal. But this suggestibility can be taken much further when the human mind (or the animal mind) enters what is usually called by the experts an ASC (Altered State of Consciousness).

Altered States of Consciousness

The human mind is capable of a variety of ASCs and it is worthwhile, before dealing with hypnosis in particular, to explain these in layman's terms so that we can see where hypnosis fits into the wider picture. ASCs can be conveniently divided into *the Natural, the Traumatic and the Induced.*

The Natural

Sleep: All humans and most higher animals experience this phenomenon regularly. We cease to be conscious of our surroundings, lie in a relaxed pose and after waking up again, usually feel refreshed.

While we are asleep we sometimes have dreams. Psychologists tell us that dreams take place for only a few seconds as we pass from deep sleep into lighter sleep, though the sleeper may well report a sense of considerable time lapse. When we are dreaming, an observer would see that our bodies twitch slightly and our eyelids flicker, and that our eyes also are in rapid motion. The dreams we remember are those we have just before awakening. In general, in a healthy person, dreams are a confused set of images which are mildly pleasant. Occasionally they are the reverse: nightmares. Sometimes these dreams will colour at least a part of the day by their vividness or emotional impact.

The Bible has several instances of dreams being of special significance as revelations from God, eg: Pharaoh's dream (Genesis 41), Nebuchadnezzar's dreams (Daniel 2, 4), Joseph's dreams (Matthew 1:20, 2:13). It is important to note that although there are a number of dreams reported in Scripture, they are reported because of their significance, not because God regularly expects us to use dreams for guidance or revelation: Ecclesiastes 5:7 (RV margin) *For in the multitude of dreams and words there are vanities.*

Day-dreams: There are a variety of lesser sleep-like ASCs: we daydream when we are relaxed, tired, or even bored. Though not unconscious, we may express this ASC when we say to someone who disturbs us, "I'm sorry, I was miles away."

The Bible may touch on this in Acts 10 (Peter's trance). For Peter, hunger mixed with the heat of the day, was enough to explain the imagery of his vision, into which God speaks with the puzzling declaration that the animals were clean. (Jesus had, in reality, already said this: Mark 7:15). The importance of the gospel to the Gentiles is amplified for Peter; the vision only served to focus what Peter already knew (Matthew 28: 'Go ye therefore and teach all nations').

The Traumatic

Fainting, shock, hysterical reactions (pleasant & unpleasant), depression, unconsciousness, coma, near-death... death.

In these examples our normal rational frame of mind becomes dislocated to a greater or lesser degree by trauma. The trauma may be emotional, physical or both. It is almost an automatic protective reaction against some form of mental or physical overload: pain, anguish, fear, horror, even humour. People usually recover from most of these (except death) – sometimes with the aid of medical intervention.

Near-death experiences.

Figures are difficult to come by, but very roughly, and depending on the cause of the experience, about 95% of them are reported as being in some sense pleasant, and about 5% as unpleasant. Little confidence should be placed in them theologically as they are inevitably highly subjective and bear little value in proving the nature of Heaven and Hell – although, unfortunately, sometimes this is done. Christians report a 'Christian' experience, Hindus a Hindu one. The one man who could have reported on a 'back from death experience'–Lazarus–never actually speaks a word in the gospels' accounts. Jesus himself, in the story of the rich man and the beggar, Lazarus, has Abraham say, "They have Moses and the prophets; let them hear them. And he said, Nay, father Abraham: but if one went to them from the dead, they will repent. And he said to him, If they hear not Moses and the prophets, neither will they be persuaded, though one rose from the dead." (Luke 16:29-31)

The Induced

Medical anaesthesia, Drug induced ecstasy, Music, Hysteria and Hypnosis.

Of anaesthesia and drug induced ecstasy very little need be said. The Bible has no positive mention of the latter, and only one instance of the former – in rather special circumstances (Genesis 2:21). In the 19th century there was debate over the correctness of using anaesthesia during child-birth (Simpson) as the method appeared to go against Genesis 3:16 – and such debates continue today with regard to child-birth, though not for theological reasons! In general few would deny, on Scriptural grounds, the great value of anaesthetics to medicine.

Music

Music is included in the list because of its power to affect emotions. Music is, of course, not necessarily wrong in and of itself. But we are open to musical suggestion, sometimes apparently against our will. How many times have you found yourself whistling or humming a tune which, in fact, you rather dislike? It is usually some irritating advertising ditty, but it has been planted in your brain and jerked into action by some chance encounter or random thought. Shopping centres appreciate the value of mood music to soothe or excite people and so make customers suggestible to impulse purchases.

But what about music used in Church services or in large Christian rallies? *Why has it become more or less indispensable?* "We must begin with a worship time," they say – by which they mean a period of singing. Why, in particular, is it a necessary feature of a 'Toronto Experience' meeting and its precursors in the Association of Vineyard Churches (AVC)?

In the New Testament *there is no evidence that any gospel preaching was accompanied by music and 'worship' beforehand.* Why has it become so essential? The answer is most likely due to its ability to infiltrate our minds and induce obedience to a rhythm or emotion outside ourselves – we can become carried away by the music – even by good music – but we mistake this experience for something spiritual, when it is in fact sensual. Naturally this is not to condemn all music in Christian meetings, but much closer examination needs to be given as to what its purpose has become.

Hypnosis and hysteria.

Both these means of inducing ASC have been practised – even if not understood – in many societies throughout the world from earliest times. They are not even unique to humans. Many predators instinctively employ techniques to generate hysteria in herds of prey or hypnotic techniques in one to one encounters. Anyone who has seen a stoat hypnotise a rabbit before attacking and killing it will know this.

From most primitive times societies have produced the shaman or priest. The shaman's function was partly to explain why things happened to the group or the individual (in terms of local spirits etc) and to be of help in times of stress. For individuals suffering pain or disease it was clearly insufficient to give explanations of suffering, it was also necessary to provide practical relief. The shaman would soon discover that people in pain were dependent and suggestible: that stories told them about 'the how and the why' could aid relief and more than that, a sense of euphoria might be induced in the sufferer by the suggestion that they now felt better. If this seems far fetched, remember your own childhood: 'mummy will kiss it better' and you stopped crying. It worked, but only for two reasons: firstly, you were dependent on your mother, and secondly, the hurt was really not very serious: rather it was the shock of the unpleasant experience that had so upset you.

It was not long before possibilities beyond simple relief of pain suggested themselves, and power over an individual or group by development of these methods followed. Thus we can envisage the 'Beast (chief) and his Prophet (priest or shaman)' gaining authority in many societies from earliest times under certain circumstances. It is important to understand that hysteria and hypnosis are co-operative phenomena: a person wants to feel better and so co-operates with the shaman, a group wants to feel powerful or happy and so co-operates with a strong leader – it is a decision of the will. Those who dissent in the heightened situation generated by hysteria or hypnosis, are at a considerable disadvantage and tend to come under group pressure to conform: most succumb.

Many detailed studies of hysteria and hypnosis have been conducted since the 18th Century and here is not the place to sketch the history of them. These ASCs have been given different names: animal magnetism, mesmerism, suggestion, hysteria, hypnotism etc. Such ASCs form the basis of most New Age and Eastern religious experiences and are part of the trickery used by fakirs and others. Much of what a gullible audience will see will not have occurred except to their suggestible minds.

The hypnotic experience

One of the problems in describing a hypnotic trance is that each individual will react differently. A hypnotist cannot predict what a subject under hypnosis will experience with any certainty. But there are a few generalisations which are worth listing.

1. Susceptibility: most people can in fact be hypnotised (even those who boast that they can't), but it does require an element of co-operation: this can be elicited by degrees and unscrupulous practitioners can achieve this by deception. As a rule the middle-classes are *more* susceptible than others: they tend to pay more attention to a situation and enter in more fully.

2. Hypnotic states vary considerably in depth: Somewhat parallel to depths of anaesthesia – the initial levels tend to be accompanied by feelings of heaviness, lightness, floating, inability to move, moving into feelings of euphoria, tingling sensations, electric currents. During this and the following stages, rapid eye movements will take place (as when dreaming) and sometimes people may report strange visions. Subjects may experience uncontrollable twitchings, laughter or tears. They may also experience automatic limb movements even without the prompting of a hypnotist. The subject will respond to physical commands, such as a pointed finger, by spasms or lying backwards. Taps on the forehead or abdomen will cause them to fall backwards. In a deep hypnotic state catalepsy can take place, where the body can become totally rigid – this effect is often used in stage performances: laying the subject with their neck resting on the back of one chair and their ankles on another and people actually walking along their totally rigid body as if along a plank.

3. Some 5% of subjects will have a bad trip: Instead of euphoria, their experience will be more like a nightmare. On being brought round, they experience ongoing problems: depression, nightmares, peculiar emotional urges and suicidal tendencies. As a rule this tends to happen to more vulnerable people.

4. Post-hypnotic suggestion: This is where hypnotism can be used to achieve apparently amazing cures. While under hypnosis, the practitioner plants particular suggestions about the subject's problem. For example, if the subject is terrified of spiders, then the practitioner suggests that the subject will not see any more spiders. And indeed this will be the case. But the effect will wear off in time. Temporary healings can be achieved by this method. They usually have to do with disorders or bad habits that are essentially mental in origin (psychosomatic illnesses): smoking, nervous coughs, stuttering, paralysis, even deafness and blindness in some cases. The *symptoms* of genuine organic disorders can often be quite effectively masked by hypnosis. Again the effect will wear off with time. Occasionally, healings can be permanent, in situations where relief of the presenting symptom allows respite to the body to enable natural healing to take place.

So far hypnotism has been described as if it were a neutral phenomenon. But what do the Scriptures have to say about it? In the Bible there are several references to hypnotism, translated as ***"charming"***.

In three places at least the charming refers to what we would call snake charming – which is a form of hypnotism (remember that animals can hypnotise and be hypnotised, this is why it is sometimes called animal magnetism)[1]. These are: "For, behold, I will send serpents, cockatrices, among you, which [will] not [be] **charmed,** and they shall bite you, saith the LORD." (Jeremiah 8:17)

"Their poison [is] like the poison of a serpent: [they are] like the deaf adder [that] stoppeth her ear; Which will not hearken to the voice of **charmers, charming** never so wisely." (Psalm 58: 4-5)

Elsewhere it is people who are 'charming' or 'being charmed' or consulting 'charmers':

"And the spirit of Egypt shall fail in the midst of her; and I will destroy her counsel: and they shall seek to the idols, and to the **charmers**, and to the mediums, and to the wizards." (Isaiah 19:3)

Most important of all is the direct prohibition to God's people against getting involved in charming:

"There shall not be found among you [any one] that maketh his son or his daughter to pass through the fire, [or] that useth divination, [or] an observer of times, or an enchanter, or a witch, Or a **charmer**, or a consulter with mediums, or a wizard, or one who calls up the dead." (Deuteronomy 18:10-11)

Thus, clearly, hypnotism is something forbidden by God *and the use of it is sinful.* In which case, any ministry which employs this technique in any way is acting contrary to God's expressed command and therefore must be avoided.

Attention will now be given to a practical comparison between secular stage hypnotism and Toronto-style meetings.

Stage hypnotism

In theory any moderately able person can be taught the technique of hypnotism of individuals or groups. Intentionally there follows only a brief summary of some of the basic requirements:

1. Co-operation: In a large group this cannot always be guaranteed: however, audiences are for the most part self-selecting: ie: those who are intrigued by hypnotism will go to the show. Stage hypnotists reckon that up to half of an audience are already lightly hypnotised by the very act of coming to the show: drawn as they may well have been by suggestive advertising.

2 Selection: In order to find the most suitable subjects for his show, the stage hypnotist must have a method of selecting the most easily hypnotised people. This he does by some such simple exercise as the following.

All present are asked to interlock their fingers, close their eyes and listen to him. He will gently tell them that their fingers are getting tighter and tighter until... he will suggest that they cannot unlock them. Most people will in fact be able to, but a proportion (say 40-50) in an average audience will find themselves unable to unlock their fingers. This phase was sometimes encouraged by 'plants' in the audience who might start audibly whispering, "help, I can't move my fingers." Again by the ripple of crowd suggestion and hysteria some, who might not otherwise succumb, will then do so. Modern shows apparently seldom bother with this and rely instead on slick hypnotic mood music, or the use of flashing lights. The practitioner works on taking hold of the will of the audience. He then selects from this group by further tests before he proceeds with the show.

3 Debriefing: After the show the hypnotist will bring the individuals concerned out of their trance by a simple command such as, "on the count of three you will return to normal".

All this sounds quite straight forward and fairly harmless: the audience have paid to come, they chose to do so, knowing–up to a point–what was expected of them.

In reality things are by no means so simple. As mentioned above, it is a statistical fact that in any group undergoing hypnosis, although about 95% come out 'successfully' with no apparent after effects, 5% do not. 95% will, under hypnosis, experience considerable degrees of euphoria, but 5% will have a 'bad trip'. Further, in a stage show, members of the audience not on the stage may also follow the stage volunteers into deep hypnosis, but, because they are not 'known subjects', these may well leave the show insufficiently debriefed.

Those 5% will suffer ongoing problems ranging from nightmares to depression and even suicidal tendencies. ***Deaths have occurred.*** [2] Naturally, stage hypnotists claim to debrief people properly, but since they are not in total control of all individuals in the audience they cannot, in fact, guarantee safety.

If this is true of stage hypnotism, then, when Toronto-type gatherings are examined, there is every reason to be extremely alarmed. *As shall be shown, there is clear evidence that hypnotism is the main feature!*

Hypnotism is responsible for the very bizarre behaviour of some individuals, the so called 'manifesting'– as we saw earlier in the section on the hypnotic experience. These correspond to the 'stage group' mentioned above. The lesser manifestations correspond to the larger group of susceptible members of the audience. However in the instance of Toronto meetings the susceptible group is a far greater proportion of the audience, because most of the people have come already lightly hypnotised by 'expectation' of what will happen to them. Their expectation is magnified by the belief that God is going to do it rather than a mere human practitioner.

It is necessary here to be very specific and name names, because this is not a neutral matter or one of mere academic interest. People are being hurt and deceived.

People such as Kenneth Copeland, Kenneth Hagin Jnr, Rodney Howard-Browne, Benny Hinn, John Arnott, together with Sandy Millar and David Pytches and many others are practising hypnotism at their meetings. On seeing the video material of their activities, anyone professionally familiar with stage hypnotism will tell you that that is what is going on.

The healings at these meetings are of the kind described above. They fade with time. The wickedness of the Faith Movement healers is that they then blame the subject for not 'keeping' their healing. In reality they cannot keep it, unless they come back for another dose of hypnotism.

It must be said that some leaders may be superficially ignorant that they are using hypnotism, but they are doing it none the less: for they have been **taught** to do it. One of the features of 'Catch the Fire' conferences is that they always include sessions for ministers on 'How to impart the blessing'.

It is probable that John Wimber and his teams have been employing hypnotism more or less from the inception of the AVC. They may not have intended this, they may in fact have hit upon the 'signs and wonders' technique almost by accident. What follows is a paper by Happy Leman from the AVC with commentary (in bold). It demonstrates that classic methods of hypnotism are being used.

VINEYARD TIPS FOR LEADERS (editor's comments in bold)

1 It is usually helpful to begin every time with worship followed by testimonies of people who have been touched. Immediately after the testimonies, invite the Holy Spirit to come upon these individuals again and do a further work. There seems to be a special grace for these people to receive another "drink" of the new wine when they are up front giving testimonies. They often begin to experience the same outward manifestations again.

COMMENT: 'Worship time' is nothing of the sort, but simply hypnotic mood music which induces compliance. The calling forward of those who succumb first to 'testify' and then 'manifest' afresh serves the purpose of further softening up of the audience for what is to follow: seeing others being hypnotised aids one's own hypnosis.

2 When ministry begins, look for those who are most obviously anointed. This can be done by looking for manifestations such as crying, shaking, laughing, etc.

COMMENT: Selection is taking place here..

3 If you don't notice any outward manifestations of the Holy Spirit, ask those who sense a strong anointing within them to come for ministry. This might manifest as a burning, tingling, "knowing," etc.

COMMENT: ...and again here.

4 Encourage people to freely receive ministry. It's OK to receive several times of prayer in the same meeting. It's also OK to receive prayer every time we gather. In fact, people seem to receive better and more fully each successive time. The more the "soaking," the deeper the impact.

COMMENT: "Encourage"; ie: suggest to an already compliant group. The more you 'soak' is the same as 'the deeper into an hypnotic state you go'.

5 Keep reassuring people that it's OK if they do not manifest anything unusual when they receive prayer. God works differently in different people. Remember to encourage people that it's not manifestations we are after but changed hearts. The manifestations are simply a by-product.

COMMENT: Reassurance is again to relax people who are, as yet, only lightly hypnotised. Manifestations are clearly not a by-product, quite the reverse. Without them nothing would be happening and the meeting utterly dull. But this suggestion implants itself in those hypnotised and forms a post-hypnotic suggestion: so people keep repeating, when challenged, that the manifestations were a by-product–despite evidence to the contrary.

6 Encourage people not to be fearful of what God is doing. This requires reassuring words from the leaders.

COMMENT: Reassuring messages encourage ASC.

7 Be willing to be prayed for yourself. People always respond best when the leaders are also responding. It seems that the leaders are the gatekeepers and what they will allow, the people feel confident to allow.

COMMENT: Here is the clear equivalent of the stage hypnotist's 'plant', or in some instances 'known pliable volunteer': demonstration always helps induce hypnosis in others.

8 Sometimes children are afraid to receive until they see their parents or other known adults receive. Some children have even been reported as being fearful of some of the manifestations they have experienced such as being pinned to the floor.

COMMENT: Children know better than adults here. It would be reprehensible, even for a stage hypnotist, to practise on children. The author has witnessed, on video, the terror of children under these circumstances.

9 Keep the "environment" light and easy. This is not a season for heavy ministry, great deliverance, or deep inner healing. It seems the Holy Spirit is emphasizing joy and release from heaviness.

COMMENT: These are classic hypnotic conditions. Feelings of lightness and pleasant heaviness are very common in hypnotic states.

10 Please refer to these manifestations as "times of refreshing" (Acts 3:19) or renewal rather than revival. Revival has the connotation of touching the larger community. Use the phrase "resting in the Spirit" rather than "slain in the Spirit."

COMMENT: This is biblical nonsense. The language difference between 'times of refreshing', 'revival' and 'renewal' in Scripture is nominal. Ananias and Sapphira were slain in the Spirit!

11 When the number of people wanting prayer is large, it seems that the quality of prayer goes down and vice versa. We've found that the people who linger around the longest and get multiple times of prayer generally get the most. Meeting and prayer times seem to move from low anointing to higher as time goes on.

COMMENT: Again these are classic conditions for hypnosis. Since when has prayer become some sort of essence which can be diluted?

Suggested Ministry Tips Happy Leman. 20th April 1994 Vineyard Christian Fellowship (Fort Wayne North)

Those who remain non-compliant are treated to a veritable battery of softening up techniques. Note the introduction of Christian medical doctors (such as Dr Patrick Dixon) [3] or Christian sociologists (such as Dr Margaret Paloma) who speak of the value of ASCs, and also of doctors of Divinity (such as Dr Mark Stibbe) [4] to 'prove' from Scripture that all is OK. Exhortations are made to 'switch off the mind', 'experience first, analyse later', all of which are standard hypnotic methodology as the following quotations demonstrate:

Above all, **do not analyse what is happening**, for this will re-activate the left-side of the brain, your reasoning conscious mind and this is the very thing you are attempting to suppress. (Emphasis in original) [5]

Do nothing – **don't think or try to analyse what is happening.** (Emphasis in the Original) [6]

Do not let your mind begin analysing or reflecting on how you are progressing with your exercises while you are engaged in carrying them out...Just launch yourself into the routine and submit or surrender yourself to the languid feeling which will result from carrying out the exercises. [7]

By now the majority of the audience is highly suggestible, so the actual content of the supposed biblical material can be of the most superficial kind. It will easily satisfy the hypnotised – they will accept anything – but utterly fail to convey any serious meaning to anyone outside the Toronto environment.

A major effect of being in an ASC is the high level of suggestibility. Or to put it another way, **the absence of discernment.**

Many years ago, when I was a pharmacology student, we undertook an experiment using a light anaesthetic (akin to laughing gas). I was the guinea pig and had to inhale whilst trying to do some simple arithmetic at the same time. Very quickly I became unable to proceed, and began to laugh. I became aware of all kinds of sounds, such as the noise of the air-conditioning, which seemed at the time as important and significant as the voices of my fellow students. I lacked any discernment as to what was important and what was not. Under hypnosis the same processes apply, which explains a curious fact about those who write favourably about their experience of Toronto meetings.

Many of the articles contain a strange mixture of relevant and irrelevant information, presented in a totally jumbled manner. They often contain surprisingly unimportant pieces of information such as the 'catchers' "were all given sticky badges"; or meeting times are given in great detail (indicating that the notices had the same apparent significance as the sermon – if there was one). Further, testimonies and arguments to support Toronto all possess a monotonous similarity: the same examples are given, even the same wording is used. More than that, odd suggestions pop up in articles such as how the participants noticed the humility of the leaders (why?), or how they were 'reassured that there was no hysteria', or that no one was pushing them over. These make sense if we accept that the writers were still actively influenced by what they were told or experienced when under hypnosis. Even though hypnotic states (and post-hypnotic suggestions) tend to fade naturally over time (unless reinforced by further sessions), those who experience Toronto are urged to write down their testimony as soon as possible. In the same paper by Happy Leman on 'Suggested Ministry Tips' – quoted above – under the heading, 'Tips when praying for people' we read the following:

12. Encourage the people you pray for to **put testimonies in written form immediately.**

Returning to the non-compliant people: these talks and the testimonies all play their part in pressurising them. Then, if this strategy fails, come the more threatening suggestions that to reject this is to reject God himself: they are 'grieving the Spirit', 'quenching the Spirit', yes even, 'blaspheming the Spirit'. Sadly, most will succumb to such pressure, especially if, as is the case in many instances, they are at the Toronto event over a period of days in a foreign country and have spent (or have had spent on them) considerable sums of money.

But what of the positive testimonies?

"I feel the love of God"

The feeling is real enough but the source is mistaken. You will feel euphoric, and many godly people will equate that perception to being loved by or having a love for God. Sadly, this is a case of mistaken identity. In 95% of cases of hypnotism, as mentioned above, euphoria is normal in anyone (godly or otherwise). This explains why non-Christian people fall down and laugh in the same way as Christians do. One problem faced by hypnotherapists is that their subjects can become addicted to this euphoria. (The euphoria has a straightforward biochemical cause. Endorphins, morphine-like chemicals, are naturally generated in the body under these conditions). One noticeable feature of Toronto Churches is the constant round of 'prayer meetings' where people go to fall down again or twitch or 'do their thing' in an attempt (usually successful) to get 'the feeling' again. The more often you indulge in self-hypnotic behaviour (as it becomes), the easier it is to achieve – in fact the sensations can quickly become addictive.

Furthermore, there is an increasing risk that, as people habitually slip into a hypnotic condition, the external aids–music, lighting, testimonies etc – will be needed less and less: then just a few skilful suggestions from the leadership will produce the desired effect. The meetings could then become even more deceptive. "Look! no mood music, no hype.. it **must** be God."

"But I was healed"

At this point we must be very blunt. Healed of what? An amputated leg? A failed kidney? Inoperable cancer? Terminal AIDS? Alzheimer's disease? Or was it something rather more nebulous? Here is a letter testifying to a healing in a Toronto style meeting:

I have been healed by the Holy Spirit, not in Toronto but at Lister Hill Baptist Church, Horsforth. One year ago I went to a meeting to hear Anne Watson speak. I did not go with the intention of receiving the Holy Spirit. Indeed, I had no idea that there would be an opportunity to do so. But later on that evening, chairs were cleared and anyone who wanted to receive was asked to move forward to the centre of the room *[ie: the now familiar 'standard procedure' for TE to begin]*.

I wanted to receive, I wanted and still want all that God has to give me *[Expectation had been greatly enhanced–classic situation for hypnotic induction]*. I knew that the only way to do that was to submit completely all my worries and fears.

I knew that the Holy Spirit was a gentleman and would not fill me if I was even slightly unsure. The result was that I kept my eyes fixed on Jesus. I found myself lying face up on the floor. I thought to myself: 'I'll just lie here and enjoy the time in the presence of God.'

But then I started to shake, especially my jaw, which shook vigorously. I was praying with my eyes fixed on Jesus all this time. I began to think, 'Is this God, or is it me being nervous?' So I asked God to stop. Almost immediately the shaking stopped. When I asked, 'More, Lord,' it began again. The Lord confirmed to me that it was He. I was safe, comfortable, rested and full of joy so close to my Lord.

[These symptoms: falling, the comfort, the fact that nothing happens 'without our permission' once we have succumbed, if we remove the wrapping, describe a standard hypnotic trance]

At one point I was afraid that my fillings would fall out. I was assured that they would not. While it was going on the Lord made it clear to me that he was healing me of a habit that I had had for 15 years, a biting of the gums to a severe degree. It had started at school through nervous tension and anxiety. No matter how hard I tried, I could not stop. I had tried everything *[including secular hypnotherapy]*. It had not occurred to me that my healing could possibly come this way.

The Lord also made it clear to me that he was healing my mouth for me to speak about what he has done in my life. The same night the chewed parts of my mouth began to heal. It was an incredible experience. It was of God, it was not just a good feeling, or me carried away by the moment.

I had been in other meetings before and since, when the Holy Spirit had come in, and I was determined that if it happened to me, God was going to have to do it. I met with God that night, that deep joy and the knowledge of his closeness to me has never left me.

I feel people should know that it is not only a good feeling that could be ascribed to any deity people were devotees of (sic). It is our almighty God and He doesn't just work in Toronto. He works all over the world and in Horsforth, Yorkshire. [8]

Unfortunately for the writer everything described here is a result of hypnotic induction: a hypnotherapist agreed that a cure for this kind of condition could be easily achieved under hypnosis. However, in this instance, the person has gone away with a serious misunderstanding about what happened to him. Incidentally, gum tissue repairs itself naturally very quickly.

In books, such as '*Catch the Fire*' by Guy Chevreau [9], there are many similar instances: the healings are all in the realm of the psychosomatic. There is much talk of inner healing etc. or being cured of dyslexia or other more ill-defined conditions. Indeed many of them could be defined as diseases of the rich Western middle classes. **All these kinds of feelings and healings are far removed from the New Testament.**

The apostles did not get up on the Day of Pentecost and talk about how they felt: they preached the gospel. Nor did the apostles ever pray 'Come Holy Spirit'.

People who were healed by Jesus, or the apostles, did not go into trances and have peculiar experiences (unless perhaps they were seen as demon possessed). Nor did they have to fear losing their healing!

When the Holy Spirit came on them people in the New Testament did not 'pogo' or twitch, or do a 'silly walk', or grunt, or do other things outside their control. They **did** speak in tongues, praise God and prophesy, **but** in a sober fashion and with alert minds. They preached the gospel clearly, served the poor, gave their lives for the faith. The reason? They were not hypnotised by men – but inspired by the Holy Spirit.

95% – 5% split

Those who get 'a good trip' are liable, in their excitement, to drown out those who do not. Add to that the guilt imputed if a person's experience was bad, and there are many in the Churches currently suffering trauma in silence: how can they speak 'against the Spirit' by saying He has damaged them? Yet they are damaged.

I am already aware of three deaths following involvement in Toronto meetings, and there are many more badly damaged people out there. "Jesus Life" magazine of the Jesus Fellowship/Jesus Army, No. 33, 3rd quarter, 1995: has an article: "The New Wine 'hangover'?" which was written a year on from their first experiences of Toronto. It speaks of "considerably less excitement" and raises the question, "Did we somehow miss the blessing?" It describes the work as "being tougher" and tells of "severe depression, marriage difficulties, and loneliness", "with a level of spiritual warfare never encountered before, and some considering quitting."

At least a stage hypnotist tries to debrief his victims. But in Churches up and down the land, people are going into trances and getting up again, driving their cars ('awfully funny' stories abound – many of them thankfully myths – of people driving in a drunken manner and being stopped by the police). It is only a matter of time before more people are killed. Church leaders cannot escape their responsibilities in this matter: yet that is precisely what they are doing. Here is an account by a journalist of his experiences at Holy Trinity Brompton (HTB) which should act as a very serious warning:

...A man in a tweed jacket with a coloured flash on his lapel, to indicate that he is one of the ministry team, asks me if I would like to pray with him. I decline this kind offer but take the opportunity to enquire what training the ministry team has. Some of the worshippers are in deep trances. What steps are taken to bring them out? "The Lord has put them in a trance. The Lord brings them out. This young lady for instance..." during the course of our conversation a young woman standing next to us has collapsed to the floor and is now lying at our feet. One acclimatises to this sort of thing remarkably swiftly. "This young lady is perfectly conscious of her surroundings. She is relaxed to listen to the Lord."

Or in English she has been hypnotised. Within an hour of leaving HTB I made careful notes of my mental and physical state and when I read them to Peter Casson of the Federation of Ethical Stage Hypnotists he confirmed what I suspected. I had felt dreamy, slow to react to outside stimulus with poor concentration ... "You would," says Peter Casson. "My art creates disassociation in the individual, so there is no contact with reality or other people..."

The golden rule is that all [stage] hypnotic suggestion should be removed before the punters go home. What about letting someone get off the floor from a deep trance and head straight for his or her car? "Reprehensible," says Peter Casson.

But this was what I witnessed at HTB. Five minutes or so after she had been lying at my feet, I saw the same young woman over whose prostrate form I had been discussing the pros and cons of trances tripping happily across the car park to drive home alone.

Bill Saunders (quoted from his article in Midweek Magazine July 1995. Used with permission.)

It is not possible to overstate the seriousness of the situation. There is no Scriptural justification for deliberately seeking out Altered States of Consciousness. Quite the contrary, Scripture contains numerous injunctions to be sober, alert and watchful, [10] particularly against being deceived. For it is when we are in some kind of ASC that deception comes most easily. **But what of the examples in Scripture of trances, visions and dreams?** Space only permits some brief comments.

Old Testament: The prophets certainly experienced visions and dreams, but several important points need to be noted.

1 They were not induced by outside stimuli: eg music (except on one occasion: 2 Kings 3:14-16), or crowd hysteria. The prophet was usually alone.

2 The experiences came to them while in prayer. Contrast this with the Toronto exhortations to stop praying!

3 They remained clearly conscious throughout.

New Testament: Eg: Acts 10. Peter, on a roof top awaiting a meal at about midday slips into a trance, where there was a clear relationship between his condition, hunger; and the nature of the vision: "Rise Peter kill and eat". He too is alone, no music, no hypnotic hype (indeed quite the reverse: the ***smell*** around Simon the tanner's house would have been most unhypnotic.)

Paul's Dream (Acts 16:9): Again, natural in nature, though divine in meaning: yet even so, Paul discusses it with Luke and the team, and only then do they all conclude that God is calling them across to Europe.

Book of Revelation: As with Daniel and one or two other apocalyptic writers, the mingling of dream, vision and writing style bears no relation to the trivial mass experiences claimed for Toronto.

Note that all these biblical instances are relatively rare: a couple of dozen over a dozen centuries is hardly an everyday event.

What about 'Slaying in the Spirit' – surely that is biblical?

It depends what you mean by biblical. If you merely mean, 'Did people fall down in the Bible?' the answer is, 'Yes.' But if you mean, 'Did people fall down in the Bible as an experience of God's blessing?' then the answer is, 'No, never.'

It is a worthwhile study to look up all the passages where people fall down in Scripture: a most interesting pattern will emerge. I am most indebted to Dr Karel Berghem who has written a most significant paper (unpublished) on this subject.

In the Bible people fall down on their faces in the presence of God, the angel of the Lord (the Lord Jesus) or an archangel. They never fall through the agency of an intermediary. *They fall as a consequence of an encounter with God.* It never occurs through the laying on of hands, the pointing of a finger or through the blowing of a human mouth.

Falling backwards takes place in cases of judgment by God or to stay the hands of God's adversaries. For example:

Genesis 49:17: 'so that his rider falls backwards'

1 Samuel 4:18: Eli fell off his seat backwards on hearing of the death of his sons and the capture of the Ark.

1 Samuel 19:23-24: The Hebrew is RUACH ELOHIM, which means spirit of God, but the grammar is identical to 1 Samuel 18:10 where it is translated, 'an evil spirit *from* God' (still RUACH ELOHIM) causes Saul to 'rave within his house'. Since in 1 Samuel 19:11, Saul is seeking to kill David we must conclude that it is the same *evil* spirit from God which afflicts him, causing him to rave again and strip off his clothes, and preventing him achieving his goal. This is judgment, not blessing!

1 Samuel 28:20: Saul falls 'full length' after hearing of his impending death after consulting the witch of Endor.

Isaiah 28:13: 'they may go and stumble backward, and be broken.'

John 18:6: 'they drew back and fell to the ground': they were coming to arrest the Son of God.

Acts 5:5,10: Judgment falls on Ananias and Sapphira.

Acts 9:4: Saul falls in judgment from Jesus as he was attempting to arrest and kill believers in Damascus.

Unlike a leaflet published by St Andrew's Anglican Church, Chorleywood which comments:

"We do not think we can establish any consistent reason why some fall

forward, some fall backward and some just crumple down on the floor. Nor do we believe that there is any sinister reason for falling backwards etc." (*What is going on? New Wine leaflet 1995*).
In fact, we can see from the Bible that it is of considerable importance how people fall!

Can 'it' be cured?

There are many testimonies of people suffering or 'enjoying' ongoing twitches, gruntings or other physical phenomena. In many cases they appear to give the person pleasure – though sometimes their spouses have had to sleep elsewhere! Such people are not very likely to immediately desire to be 'cured'. Further, the experiences are decidedly habit forming. The long term spiritual damage is very obvious, the psychological and physical damage more difficult to predict.

Those who will have been directly damaged by TE may well want help, but they too face barriers. To whom can they turn for help? Their own "Torontoed" Church would clearly blame them. It would take courage to look elsewhere.

How can they be helped? A hypnotherapist would say that these people are essentially damaged because they were not properly debriefed. The reality may not be as simple as that – it has become apparent that hypnotism opens the mind not just to improper suggestions, but to a spirit world forbidden by God's Word. Repentance of involvement in Toronto should be sufficient to deliver people from unpleasant (or even pleasant) symptoms of hypnotic suggestion. But even if there are no specific symptoms, we do need to repent of our involvement in these things.

Deliverance ministry in this context should be treated with great caution, as this could lead back into the shamanism Christians need to reject! People often become irrationally angry when challenged over Toronto. It might be easy to assign this anger to a 'demon'. Generally this is unhelpful. The anger is more likely caused by the internal conflict of the victim: post-hypnotic suggestions suppress the reason and the will by a form of self-deception. This conflict within is probably enough to explain the irrational anger – they are literally in two minds.

Further, a strange effect that often occurs after experiencing ASC is a form of amnesia. We are familiar with this naturally, when we occasionally try to remember a dream which we enjoyed, but have lost. It can occur in a more serious way when people suffer from concussion, or after a *petit mal* attack. A sufferer can sometimes deny point blank that any such event has occurred. The same can occur after hypnosis (even self-induced hypnosis). Toronto supporters can be shown some of the appalling video material of meetings and appear not to see it – even if they were personally involved in some of the bizarre scenes.

Conclusion

Sadly, without doubt, the Toronto/Wimber/Faith movements are based on a deception. The 'signs and wonders' are in fact nothing of the kind and are certainly not from God. *Christians must not be gullible,* yet many Christian people seem to be. Perhaps, for some of us, our very middle-class upbringing is our downfall. We believe that people are basically well-meaning (Could it be we have imbibed too much Winnie the Pooh philosophy in our childhood?). This gullibility is what some of the leaders of these movements can use to their advantage. If we don't believe that wolves exist, then wolves need not even bother with sheep's clothing! Yet the Bible is full of warnings against deception. It is starkly realistic when it states that 'all have sinned', that 'the heart is deceitful above all things and desperately wicked: who can know it?' (Jeremiah 17:9) 'If we say that we have no sin we deceive ourselves...' (1 John 1:8) But let us accept the gracious forgiveness of God as we repent of these things:

'If we confess our sins, He is faithful and just to forgive us our sins and cleanse us from all unrighteousness.' **1 John 1:9**

Notes

1 Even a dog can hypnotise humans according to a report in the **Daily Mail,** 27th October 1995.

2 **Campaign against Stage Hypnotism:** 62 Station Rd, Hesketh Bank, Nr Preston, Lancs PR4 6SP

3 **Signs of Revival, Dr Patrick Dixon**, Kingsway 1994

4 **Times of Refreshing, Dr Mark Stibbe,** Marshall Pickering 1995

5 **Autohypnosis, R.Shone** 1982: p.45

6 **The Theory and Practice of Hypnotism, W.Ousby** 1990: pp.162 163

7 ibid. p.131

8 Correspondence in **CEN** during Oct 1995. The correspondent subsequently stated that they had tried a hypnotherapist earlier who had failed to cure her. I would suggest that it was 'second time lucky'. Belief systems affect response to hypnosis. The feeling of guilt over using secular hypnosis would, of course, contribute to failure, but also sensitise the person for the next time, when the 'godly' atmosphere would not trigger the guilt.

9 'Catch the Fire' Guy Chevreau, Marshall Pickering 1994

10. See for example: **Matthew 24:4, 26:41, Mark 13:33 & parallels, Acts 20:28, Ephesians 6:18, Galatians 5:23, Philippians 3:2, Colossians 4:2, 1Thessalonians 5:6,8, 1Timothy 4:16, Titus 2:6, 1Peter 1:13, 4:7, 5:8, 2John 1:8.**

Books:

'The Toronto Blessing: Slaying in the Spirit, The Telling Wonder**' Nader Mikhaiel**
ISBN 0 646 125745

'The Serpent and the Cross' Alan Morrison, 1994 K&M ISBN 0 9523041 0 4. Although I do not agree with every aspect of this book, in my view Morrison's underlying thesis is sound and the book a vital resource.

'Words, Wonders and Power' Martyn Percy, 1996 SPCK ISBN 0 281 04855 X. A scholarly assessment of the sociology of power within the Vineyard Churches.

Old heresies, new clothes

Peter Glover

Since the days of the early Church, Christians have debated whether prophecy, in the form of new revelation, and miracle-working, in the form of signs and wonders performed by believers, still have a place in the life of the Church. Christians, generally speaking, tend to view new revelation and signs and wonders collectively. They view them either as clear dual realities meant only for the formative, early Church or as dual realities for the Church in every age.

The Purpose of Signs & Wonders

The purpose of this book and this section is, primarily, to look at the nature and purpose of *biblical* signs and wonders. Inevitably, however, we will touch on the whole issue of new revelation. The bond that ties these two inextricably is our individual view of the supernatural and the fact that Scripture links them together.

Let me say immediately that this part of the book, and indeed the book as a whole, is not for the Christian who has already ruled a 'wonder-working God' out of court. Those who cannot believe that our Lord can and does break into the 'natural' world in a supernatural and miracle-working way, and has done so throughout history, will find nothing to support their case here. It seems to me a small thing whether God does or does not perform miracles – having created the miracle of the universe, anything else, including the raising of the dead, would be simple for Him in comparison.

Miracles, for me as for the other contributors here, are not a big issue. As C.S. Lewis pointed out to all mature Christians, "Miracles are for beginners." For each of us, it is *truth* which is the much greater issue. The very reason for writing this book is that all of the authors believe that the dearest need in the Church today is for sound biblical, spiritual discernment. It is my contention that spiritual discernment is at an all-time low in today's Church. Christians have become increasingly ignorant about the supernatural and the devil's abilities, to the point where naive spiritual credulity has taken over. Hence we have spiritual chaos and an increasing inability in the Church to know what is, and what is not, of God.

The chief objective of this book then is not to debate whether God can, or even does, perform miracles – *that is already assumed.* (I explicitly state the case here because far too many Christians today assume that those who believe *biblical* signs and wonders were never intended to be on-going in the life of the Church, also do not believe in a miracle-working God. *Nothing could be further from the truth.) All* of the authors of this book believe in a wonder-working God who parted the Red Sea, raised our Lord *bodily* from the dead and, from time to time, still breaks into the 'natural' run of things in a 'supernatural' way. The real issue – and above all else in this debate, this needs to be understood – is not 'miracles' *performed by God*, the issue is signs and wonders (mostly miracles, but not exclusively miracles) *performed by men.* Our sole interest here is not geared to man's view of signs and wonders – but to the nature of 'signs and wonders' as revealed in the Bible.

This controversy has engaged the Church on a number of significant occasions since the days of the apostles. There is nothing new in the debate which, once again, rages in our day. The thing that is new today, however, is the scale of the split over the issue, particularly in the evangelical wing of the Church. Many Christians have now come to believe that signs and wonders are a necessary and vital aspect of the gospel itself. Without it, they say, the gospel is 'robbed of its power'. We need first to understand fully the implications of such a view. Without raw shows of God's power in tandem with the *message* of the gospel, it is being maintained that the gospel has no real power. Such belief, in fact, turns on its head orthodox Christian belief right back to the time of Jesus Himself. Orthodox Christian belief and the fathers of the Church throughout history have taught something quite different – that the Holy Spirit is in the message itself, *enabling* the very act of believing. Put another way, the real power of God is revealed in the message of the gospel itself. It is the very enabling power of the Holy

Spirit that brings about faith in believers and all that flows from it.

The advent of Pentecostalism, followed by the Charismatic Movement and then the 'Third Wave' (John Wimber and the Vineyard teaching) has made massive in-roads into biblical evangelical belief and practice. The most visible outworking of all of this today has been the 'Toronto Blessing' and the rise of an array of 'anointed', 'end-time' prophets with their alleged new revelations from God and an apparent ability to perform signs and wonders.

Debates in the modern Church have centred on the nature and meaning of new 'movements of the Spirit'. The fruit of all of this is, undoubtedly, leading the Church to a new ecumenical unity, with the ultimate goal of a visibly unified Church. We are already seeing inter-faith activity on a scale unprecedented since the Reformation. But this unity is not based on truth as defined by the doctrines (teachings) of the faith in our Bibles. For many today it is a unity forged on the basis of a common or shared manifested or physical experience of God – power encounters and phenomena. What we are seeing is a wholesale turning away from the perceived 'divisiveness' of Scriptural teaching. Historically, we are told, the visible unity of the Church has not been achievable because the doctrines of Scripture are divisive. Such observations are, of course, entirely accurate – historically, God's truth has always been difficult to accept, even by believers. Consequently, those who hold to Scriptural truths, as the eternal and unchanging Word of God, are labelled 'nit-pickers', 'heresy-hunters' and 'legalists' (for holding to doctrinal truths – what Jesus calls 'obeying my commandments'). The authors of this book would, no doubt, be described by some in this way for having the temerity to question them. Yet it was Jesus Himself who said, "He who has My commandments and keeps them, it is he who loves Me." (John 14:21). It is a sobering thought that each of us will be held accountable for what we personally choose to believe or ignore. It will be no defence to say "My leader said so...."

In Jesus' constantly reiterated reminders that it is only those who keep His commandments who are in truth proving their love for Him, do we find the real secret of the lack of spriritual discernment in the Church today. The test of whether we are obeying and loving our Lord is: *are we conforming our lives to the commandments and doctrines of the faith delivered to us through the Scriptures?* Jesus' death on the cross has not changed the requirement to observe God's commandments one iota. We may find it easy to abide by 'do not murder' or 'do not steal', because these commandments are also paralleled by non-acceptance within society. But how do we fare when faced with dealing with idols in our lives (ie being hooked on the lottery) or honouring our father and mother or observing the sabbath. Do we take this with a pinch of salt? – because these commandments are as relevant today as ever they were under the old covenant. The fact is, we will still keep the principle of observing the sabbath and resting from our work one day in seven – if we love Him. The moral law of God still stands today as much as ever, and it will eternally.

There is a gross misunderstanding today that we are no longer subject to the commandments or to doctrine. The fact is we are no longer *justified* by observing the law as in OT days. Neither are we, therefore, subject to the *penalty* of the law. Christ crucified changed all that. But, as Jesus so often reiterated, it is by the very act of obeying the commandments, out of love for Him, that we prove our love is real – ie: we do not obey His commandments because we have to, but because we want to! We have a choice. 'Having to' would indeed be legalism, 'wanting to' observe His commandments because we love Him and want to please Him, is most certainly not legalism. The choice remains ours. How many today are failing to understand this? If our lives do not conform to the commandments and doctrines of the whole of Scripture then what does 'living by faith' mean? For many today it means living supernaturally via the latest supernatural experience, believing it to be the 'work of the Holy Spirit'. Antinomianist's (those who are 'anti-law') believe we are no longer subject to God's moral laws, because we live 'by the Spirit' ie: directed 'from within' not 'from without'– by God's Word in Scripture. They have failed to understand the nature of the transition from the Old to the New Covenant. No wonder, in our day, Gnostic mysticism – experientially based Christianity – is once again rearing its ugly head. Are we so quick to forget that the very reason many of our NT books were written was to combat such counterfeit, super-spiritual Christianity?

It should at this stage be openly stated that the four authors do not see experience as unimportant or irrelevant. A genuine 'experience' of God may often be a method used by God to get our attention. None of us despises the true experiences of others. Indeed, to know the doctrines of the faith (ivory-tower dogmatism) without experiencing their reality through the presence of the Holy Spirit would be an equal and opposite error. All of us, however, know only too well that experience is also subjective – while the objective truths laid down in Scripture are eternal. Put another way, we walk by faith, not by sight (ie: *not by experience through the senses*). We do not need to 'see things happen'. We believe because of the witness of Jesus and the apostles, not because we got 'zapped' by an experience in Church last week. Scripture contains their legacy – the foundation of the Church itself. There is no other source of truth available to us. If a prophet or apostle spoke in history it could always be checked by Scripture. If a so-called prophet speaks today he or she will often believe that his/her private insight from God is above questioning. That is why any experience – even those anointed, taken up to heaven, Spirit-filled, end-time prophets – must always be brought to the bar of Scripture to be tested to see whether what is said is of God or not. The reverse, bringing the teachings (doctrines) of the faith, to the bar of our subjective experience or private revelation, is simply downright dangerous, because of Satan's real ability to counterfeit experience. That way lies deception, delusion and the real danger of apostasy. Most important, *the Scriptures themselves specifically warn us of this.*

Many who hold to the truths contained in the Scriptures, *which they know to be divisive*, already believe that the 'invisible' Church is already unified across denominational lines – based on acceptance of Scriptural truth, particularly on matters relating to salvation issues. They believe, as I do, that searching for a visible, ecumenical unity is a 'red herring' and can *only* be attained at the cost of truth. We are seeing this in our day in a host of new movements. We need to remember that when Jesus preached hard truths to his hearers they often left in droves. Hard truths are never popular, the road to visible unity simply removes those hard truths.

One thing is certain, there is no middle road. For all of the heated debate on these matters one of the central issues today revolves around signs and wonders. It seems to each of us (the writers) that this whole issue is underpinning many of the beliefs, practices and movements in the modern Church as we approach the third millennium. It is essential then that we understand the nature and purpose of signs and wonders – or, put more simply, how God has worked and is working among us.

One's view of the nature of signs and wonders today will almost certainly colour one's whole view of the new alleged movements of the Spirit in the contemporary Church. Most important of all, however, is that the Bible itself warns us that the matter of signs and wonders, and thus the supernatural, is the very issue that will create major problems for the Church in the last days.

So then, let us look closely at what the Scriptures – the Word of God – have to say on the subject.

A Biblical Overview

Most of the events depicted in the Bible as 'signs and wonders' are miraculous, though not all. According to Jesus, John the Baptist was the greatest prophet that ever lived, and yet he never performed a single miracle. It is clear that signs and wonders – as the Bible refers to them – only appear to be clustered around particularly significant symbolic events that are part of God's historical and redemptive process for man. They were all also performed through the hands of chosen men. Equally, signs and wonders were performed in conjunction with periods of new revelational truth being revealed by God, ie: they went with a new message. This is central for an understanding of signs and wonders as presented to us in the biblical context.

In the whole of the Old Testament, nowhere are signs and wonders more apparent than in the events surrounding the Exodus. So profound was the Exodus and the 'signs and wonders' attached to it, that later generations of Israelites regularly harked back to it. Stephen reminded hearers, "He brought them out, after he had shown wonders and signs in the land of Egypt, and in the Red Sea, and in the wilderness forty years." (Acts 7:36)

This is the only event in the Old Testament that attracts such a vast array of witnesses testifying to signs and wonders. There are many other biblical references to individual miracles, but these are not referred to as, and do not fit the pattern of, *biblical signs and wonders*. I cannot better Don Carson's explanation of the significance of biblical signs and wonders, which I record again here: "When 'signs and wonders' refers to God's major redemptive-historical appointments, what function do such references have in the texts where they are found? One of their major purposes is to *call the people of God back to those foundation events, to encourage them to remember God's saving acts in history, to discern their significance, and to pass on that information to the next generation*" (italics mine).

He refers to Deuteronomy 6:20-24 to support this view: "When your son asks you in time to come, saying, 'What is the meaning of the testimonies, the statutes, and the judgments which the Lord has commanded you?' then you shall say to your son: 'We were slaves of Pharaoh in Egypt, and the Lord brought us out of Egypt with a mighty hand; and the Lord showed signs and wonders before our eyes, great and severe, against Egypt, Pharaoh, and all his household. Then He brought us out from there, that He might bring us in, to give us the land of which He swore to our fathers. And the Lord commanded us to observe all these statutes, to fear the Lord our God, for our good always, that He might preserve us alive, as it is this day."

Carson continues with a vastly important and incisive statement when he says, "Unbelief in Israel is nothing other than the reprehensible forgetting of all the wonders God performed at the Exodus (Psalms 78: 11-12; 106:7) by contrast, the psalmists extol God by calling to mind the redemptive deeds of the Lord (eg: Psalms 77:11, 15; 105:5)."[1]

In a nutshell, God has drawn vivid attention, by His performance of signs and wonders through men, to significant events in the redemptive–historical process (putting man right with Him) *which He would have us remember.* The next time we meet with such a plethora of activity in the form of signs and wonders is in conjunction with the saving work of our Lord and the activity of the apostles, in building the foundation of the Church.

Signs & Wonders in the New Testament

The most significant feature of the signs and wonders we find in the pages of the New Testament is that far from being merely displays of God's power, they are as Carson points out, "...symbol-laden events rich in meaning for those with eyes to see."[2] When Jesus turned the water into wine at the wedding in Cana it was not just a magic trick. Any old wine would have done for that. But it was the best wine. It revealed the very best of what God can give to His children. Many other miracles were performed by Jesus, not as magic tricks, there were already enough magicians doing the rounds performing those; they were performed, primarily to attest to who He (Jesus) was and to draw attention to the message He brought. Without the message, the act of raw power was meaningless.

For this reason Jesus consistently refused to comply with the request to 'perform a trick'. He went much further and chastised those that wanted Him to do so. "This is a wicked generation. It asks for a miraculous sign, but none will be given it except the sign of Jonah" (Luke 11:29). Again, he reminds them that belief depends upon past acts rather than on-going, contemporary proofs. Their very expectation (as today?) was wrong. Is there any clearer parallel to the 'miracle-seekers' Jesus chides, than those in the modern signs and wonders movement?

Many of us would expect Jesus, as the Son of God, to have no trouble performing miraculous signs and wonders. We must, however, hang on to the fact that they were never just raw acts of power, they were symbolic and rich in meaning. The real debate, however, comes when we turn our attention to those who can actually perform them.

The Acts of the Apostles

It is my assertion here that the acts specifically labelled 'signs and wonders' in the New Testament were only ever performed by apostles and by a select few in the immediate apostolic company (eg: Stephen, a Deacon) in the days of the early Church.

The fact is clearly that apostles were confirmed prophets, healers, preachers and teachers who acted as spokesmen of God's infallible

Word to the newly-founded, baby Church. It is their teachings which form the body of the Church's only foundational documents, the corpus of New Testament writings. As Peter himself points out (and as Luther constantly reminded those who sought after spectacular experience and new revelation): "We also have the prophetic word *made more sure*, which you will do well to heed as a light that shines in a dark place, until the day dawns and the morning star rises in your hearts." (2 Peter 1:19)

What we have here is a vital indication that Scripture is prophecy made more sure. Put another way, Scripture will always outrank private or personal revelation – this is our permanent guide until the final stage of God's redemptive-historical process: the return and second coming of Jesus. These words, our Scriptures, were to be written down by chosen apostles. These were men who, like Jesus, would be attested by meaningful, symbol-laden and powerful signs and wonders. Who would have listened to them had they not had incredible signs that showed God was with them? They did not yet have the collective witness and testimony of New Testament Scripture.

This extraordinary period of God's new historical-redemptive act would, when completed, form the basis of the collective teaching of the apostles and our New Testament Scriptures. These alone would provide the information necessary for us to find faith in Christ. The dictum of the Reformers applies: (by whose name can we be saved?) *Christ alone*, (how are we to be justified before God?) *faith alone*, (where does the Church's authority lie?) *Scripture alone*.

We are not called to expect on-going signs and wonders. The sign-gifts were for a very specific purpose and attached to a very specific office – that of apostle. Why on earth would we need them today? Their purpose has long since been fulfilled. For faith to be faith, it cannot be allowed to rest on miracles and experiences – especially when most miracles and experiences can be counterfeited by Satan. "As Satan is 'the father of lies' (John 8:44), we are to arm ourselves with truth, not experience. As marvellous and assuring as Christian experience often is, it can be easily duplicated by the devil, and its subjectivity renders it vulnerable in battle."[3]

True & False Signs & Wonders

Many Christians are only too ready to equate the supernatural with the divine. The Scriptures specifically warn us against such a practice. Every Christian has been warned, through the Scriptures, that the supernatural is not just the province of the Father. In Scripture we have regularly been warned to beware of false and lying prophets and wonder-workers – even those who claim to act in God's name. Remember that the Egyptian magicians could match Moses miracle for miracle for a significant time. (Exodus 7:8 - 8:18) The supernatural is not just the province of God, it is also very much where Satan does his 'best work'. It is part of our function to be able to distinguish *who* is behind the supernatural activity. In doing so, we have certainly not been left as 'orphans' – our Father has more than given us the ability to spiritually discern and thoroughly 'test all things'.

Simon Magus (from where we get our word 'magician') was a worker of wonders. It was only when he came face to face with the real thing, wrought through the hands of the apostles, that he saw what he had was a counterfeit – the power was simply not in the same league. This is central in understanding the nature of what passes for signs and wonders in today's Church. The fact is the power at work in the Churches of today's signs and wonders movement is just not in the same league. Note the droves of temporary and psychosomatic 'healings' and match them against the incredible wonders wrought in Jesus' day and the days of the early Church.

If, in accepting virtually anything supernatural as the activity of God, many in the new Christian experience-based movements are reacting to a dead formalism that questions a miracle-working God, then the charge laid against them must be one of naivete. Put more bluntly, many Christians are being drawn into a mystical Christianity with all the hallmarks of early Church gnosticism (Greek *gnosis* – meaning a secret or higher knowledge).

From the start we need to note who it was that actually performed signs and wonders in the early Church. The Bible tells us clearly: *signs and wonders in the early Church were performed only by the hands of the apostles*, and by the immediate apostolic company. Let us look at the Scriptures:

"Everyone was filled with awe, and many wonders and miraculous signs were done *by the apostles.*" (Acts 2:43)

"*The apostles* performed many miraculous signs and wonders among the people....As a result, people brought the sick into the streets and laid them on beds and mats so that at least *Peter's* shadow might fall on some of them as he passed by......and **all of them** were healed." (Acts 5:12-16)

"These things *that mark an apostle* – signs, wonders and miracles – were done among you with great perseverance." (2 Corinthians 12:12)

What should be noted above all else is this: the evidence in Scripture reveals that it was always *and only* the apostles and a select few attached to their company who were able to perform signs and wonders. There is certainly no evidence that anyone else had this ability. Any other view is, quite simply, to go beyond what the Scriptures actually teach. I would describe it this way – God manifested certain powers through these men that are not manifested to others. Further, these powers clearly marked out those who held the office of apostle. In addition, please note, that *all* who were brought to them were healed. As with Jesus there was no rate of failure when His chosen few were performing what the Bible calls signs and wonders. How does that compare with the feeble attempts at modern claims to heal the sick through wonder-working believers today? And I am not here speaking of healing through prayer and through God's sovereign will – I am directly referring to alleged modern prophets and apostles *as they will.*

Clearly, what marks an apostle is the ability to perform signs and wonders. Anyone then who lays claim to the office of apostle (and there are many today) *must* be able to perform signs and wonders as did the apostles in the early Church – and with the same 100% rate of success *when they were performing what the Scriptures refer to as signs and wonders*, ie: linked to a powerful, symbol-laden and foundational, revelational message of truth for the new expression of the Church. The success rate should not be disregarded. Note again: Acts 5: 15/16 tells us that when the apostles' work was at its height, the sick and tormented were brought into the streets and '*all of them* were healed' (italics mine). But there's more. Note also that on later occasions, when the message was not the key issue and no new revelation was involved, it was not always possible for the apostles to bring healing even when that healing was for close friends. Paul tells us "I left Trophimus sick in Miletus". He told Timothy to take a little wine for his stomach's sake (clearly he was often unwell). Paul had his own thorn in the flesh (probably physical, though possibly not). No healing here then. What do we glean from this? Well, certainly that it is no part of God's work to heal everybody at the beck and call of apostles or any other so-called anointed leaders. Signs and wonders were clearly, even in the early Church, only ever performed *at the hands of men* where they served the new revelational message they accompanied *and never at other times*.

It is important also to note that this does *not* mean God does not act miraculously from time to time – clearly He did and still does, often in response to our prayers. But that is vastly different in nature from *men* performing signs and wonders. But in all of this we really must understand that it is the Scriptures alone which tell us what is meant by signs and wonders. God is sovereign and acts accordingly when it comes to the miraculous. So much then for tapping into a 'force of faith' at will as preached by modern day heretics such as Benny Hinn, David (formerly Paul)Yonggi-Cho, Morris Cerullo and Kenneth Copeland. What must be remembered is that the act of divine power pointed to the revelational message and the revelational message and wonder-working were both 100% true and complete. Anything less and it cannot be from God.

God does not make mistakes when He speaks prophetically giving new revelation, though many today claim it can be up to 35% faulty (and that, in time, we will improve they say). As one writer puts it 'would you really fly in a plane that has a 35% chance of crashing?' – well, neither should you trust a prophecy that has a third of a chance of not being from God at all or a wonder-working apostle whose success rate is less than the average hospital casualty ward.

The Old Testament prophets and the New Testament apostles *never* got it wrong when they were speaking God's infallible Word. The result is our Scriptures. Of course, they made mistakes at other times – they were still human. But when God specifically spoke new revelation through them they could only speak *that which He gave them*. They did not interpret what was said – they merely repeated it. Hence Peter could say, "Above all, you must understand that no prophecy of Scripture came about by the prophet's own interpretation." (2 Peter 1:20) A prophet/apostle could only ever speak prophetically and revelationally what he was given – if it were any other way, we would not be able to trust it completely. The old chestnut that is trotted out in defence of the theory of partial error in all prophecy is the confrontation of Paul by Agabus. It is said that Agabus got his facts wrong in saying that Paul would be bound by the Jews of Jerusalem who would hand him over to the Gentiles. They say it was the Romans who literally bound Paul. This is true. But he was bound *because* of the Jews of Jerusalem, it was they who were responsible. Agabus got it right.

Some today say that signs and wonders cannot be performed because we live in an unbelieving world which inhibits the supernatural. But how much more unbelieving was the world that the early Church apostles operated in? There are millions of Christian believers today, and the problem with the supernatural is that people are only too willing to be caught up with it. Just look at how many (including Christians) read their horoscopes daily, go to yoga classes, are caught up in the New Age psychology movements with its spurious philosophies.

And yet, there are clearly people around today, many of whom are *inside* the Church, who do claim to perform signs and wonders. But, if we take the trouble to assess a little more closely we might note that the ability to perform signs and wonders in the modern Church certainly does have identifiable hallmarks. Earlier in these pages (Mark Haville's section) you will have read of the atmosphere-creation abilities central to the work of hypnotists and now to that of some Church leaders. In church circles we are seeing the 'curing' of pyschosomatic illnesses – a distinct feature of the occult, hypnotherapy and other religions. Equally, in church circles, we are witnessing the inability to deal with major illnesses like AIDS and congenital deformity. We hear of the humiliation of believers who resort to barking like dogs and making animal noises – God's humiliation of Nebuchadnezzar is the nearest biblical equivalent. We hear of Christian leaders requiring believers not to analyse – just to experience, when the Scriptures teach *the exact opposite*: "Beloved, do not believe every spirit, but test the spirits, whether they are of God; because many false prophets have gone into the world." (1 John 4:1) Let us add: "Therefore be serious and watchful in your prayers." (1 Peter 4:7) "Be sober, be vigilant" (1 Peter 5:8) and "Let us not sleep, as others do, but let us watch and be sober." (1 Thessalonians 5:6) How many times do we have to be told? Surely God is entitled to be not a little 'miffed' at the mindlessness being touted as 'spiritual' experience today.

Anti-intellectualism is rife in the Church. It is a response to the rationalisation of liberal Christianity. But it is mistaken. It is not intellectualism that we seek, but we are called to be 'renewed through our minds' (Romans 12:2). It is indeed a hallmark of the Signs & Wonders Movement today that its success depends on those present emptying their minds, not praying, not listening to Scripture and being caught up in a manufactured atmosphere, totally dominated by the leader. If you have been to signs and wonders meetings, as I have, it is common to hear 'don't pray, do that later and don't think, just drink'. I cannot think of a more direct route to let the devil get a foothold. These meetings need big groups and troublesome Christian doctrine must be rooted out for the evening to succeed in its experience-seeking. It needs mindlessness, not alertness, to succeed – exactly the same attributes that have been openly used by hypnotists, sorcerers (see Philip Foster's section) and modern signs and wonders practitioners (see Mark Haville's section) alike.

If you think, in common with many of the leaders of these movements, that judging by the fruit is all we can do, you would be wrong. Certainly, we can judge by fruit as Matthew 7:16 clearly tells us. But there are many ways of testing, and fruit can take a long time to fully ripen. Many of the writers here are very aware of the increasing numbers of depressions and other psychological illnesses being experienced by those who have come off their temporary high after they got involved with the 'Toronto Experience'. Chris Hand's section is particularly valuable in testing biblically (the *only* method we in the church have when it comes to belief and practice) the alleged fruit of the Toronto Experience. It does not take much consideration to understand that so many things can damage us if we sink ourselves into them and try them out first. In so many areas such a philosophy would be unthinkable. Would we take heroin to test it, or do we rely on the word of medical science and other observable evidences that it is bad for us? Clearly the 'fruit' of testing heroin directly would be extremely dangerous. There must be other helpful ways, and there are. The experience of others relating to the inherent dangers in all drugs is a good and valid indicator. The same applies to new movements and their leaders. God expects us to test them: "He who is spiritual judges all things." (1 Corinthians 2:15). As has been said, there are many ways of testing. If you knew there was a blight on the land in May, would you be wise to wait until September to see what fruit would appear? A good farmer can often tell what fruit will appear *by the nature of the roots.*

Testing by the roots can be difficult, because roots are often well covered. Roots need uncovering. After all, "A good tree cannot bear bad fruit, nor can a bad tree bear good fruit." (Matt. 7:18) If the theology of a movement is bad – then so will any movement which is borne of it be bad – as time will tell (all of the authors have come across examples of pyschological damage among those who submitted to the 'Toronto Blessing' and similar experiences).

The issue of healing has been at the forefront of the modern Signs and Wonders Movement. We have been told that God wants to heal everybody of ailments and that we have it in our power to take control and, through faith, we can demand that the sickness 'depart'. Certainly I would accept that where there is sickness we can always pray for good health to be restored – but that is a very different thing from taking control and having power to demand the person be made well. None of us possesses that gift or ability today. God may well intervene through our praying, but healing is a matter that falls within His sovereignty to administer, not our province to demand. Neither do we 'tear down strongholds' in the heavenlies or 'take the ground' or claim victory over demons. Where do we read of the apostles using these expressions?

It should also be quite clear that God often uses sickness to achieve His own ends. The classic example is, of course, Job. It is equally clear that sickness can be a major benefit in God teaching us to trust Him or understand much greater truths. Benny Hinn would have palpitations at that last statement. Hinn often blames Job for causing his own problems through 'negative confessions'. The Bible paints exactly the opposite picture. Hardship often refines like gold. Paul was 'given' a thorn in the flesh which was probably an illness to 'keep his feet on the ground' when he had been richly blessed by God. David had cause to say, "It is good for me that I have been afflicted" (Psalm 119:71). Job was severely tested by illnesses – and God stood back and allowed it.

If that is not convincing, think then about the whole nature of healings that take place at the hands of our signs and wonders friends, with the heavy emphasis on physical sensations. There is no evidence of this in Scripture. People were never only partially healed by Jesus and the apostles. If healing was taking place, then they were completely and immediately healed – and of chronic, and congenital illnesses. Remember the man born blind? Do note the strong disparity between the nature of biblical healings and the nature of the modern day experience at the hands of so-called modern wonder-workers. Listen to the words of a well-loved Christian doctor on this subject:

"If there is a lot of talk about the physical aspect of the experience or excitement about it, we should always be extremely suspicious.....Once again, of course, we must remember that the evil spirits can also heal – there is no doubt about that. For every case that you can produce of spiritual healing as the result of the influence of the Holy Spirit, the spiritists, or spiritualists, whichever you like to call them, can produce an equal number of cases....How then do we tell the difference?....You will find in the case of the spiritist healings that *there is always emphasis on the physical element.* (italics mine) People will testify to a feeling of heat as the hand of the healer came upon them, or a sensation like an electric shock or something like that – the physical is always very prominent.....but there is nothing corresponding to that in the New Testament...But here, you see, the devil once more falls into the same trap. He always overdoes things, making it spectacular – too spectacular – and he calls attention to the physical concomitants." [4] So says Dr Martin Lloyd-Jones.

Does this ring any bells with the kind of Christian healing meetings you may have attended? Such an emphasis on the physical is present in all faith healing. It is, perhaps also worth noting something else missing from Scripture – that *no one ever collapsed when Jesus or the apostles laid hands on them.*

In the introduction to the same book quoted above, Lloyd-Jones' grandson Christopher Catherwood provides another helpful insight into his grandfather's understanding of signs and wonders: "Phenomena," my grandfather once told a group of doctors, "must never determine belief." One should only believe what Scripture clearly taught, and examine all unusual occurrences in its light. "Be open," he would say, "be ready to listen, but never uncritical." Wise words for our day.

In his fine book *Signs of the Apostles* Walter Chantry says, "The gift of healing serves to enhance the authority of the one who has the gift. Great numbers believe the opinions of those who perform wonders because their 'gifts' indicate that 'they are filled with the Spirit.' The implication of such logic is clear. How can anyone question the doctrine of miracle-workers? Even if one were to reason from the Scriptures, he would have no miracles to support his position. Many prefer to trust the teachings of men because of their 'gifts'. 'Can a man be teaching false doctrine when he does such mighty things, ask the captivated." [5]

The answer clearly is 'yes'. How many times did the New Testament writers warn us about lying signs and wonders? They could not have been clearer. The major point to remember is that this is a warning to those *inside* the Church that others *inside* the Church, will become deluded in their understanding of the supernatural and the working of lying signs and wonders – allegedly in the name of God – and will deceive many into joining them in their delusion.

John Wimber's Vineyard Movement

Which brings us naturally to the major contemporary proponents of modern signs and wonders, John Wimber and the Vineyard Movement. I do not propose to engage in a full appraisal of the teaching of the Vineyard. That has been done well enough elsewhere. It is necessary, however, to mention the most salient aspects of belief in this area of signs and wonders.

Let me preface what I say here by acknowledging what everybody says about Wimber – that he is a nice man. I wish I had a pound for every time the focus of an 'appraisal' is on how 'nice', how 'humble', or how 'godly' he or she seemed to be. What all of us should be deeply interested in is, as a very public Christian leader, what is he or she *actually teaching*, not how 'nice' they are. I understand that Adolf Hitler could be perfectly charming in the flesh. I am sure 'love' and 'relationships' were also high on his personal agenda – the problem was he cared nothing for truth. 'Love' and 'relationships', the watchwords in the modern Church, are actually valueless if they are not based on truth – and truth means Christ and his teachings.

I have no doubt that Wimber is genuine in his belief. This applies to many others engaged upon error. The fact that you genuinely believe the road you are on will not take you over a cliff, does not change the *truth* that it will. Wimber does not believe that healings or miracles will take place every time. But, he does believe that Christians should expect signs and wonders as surely as they should expect conversions. Signs and Wonders, he believes, confirm the Christian's faith and are necessary manifestations of the Kingdom's presence and advance. He believes that evangelism and the sharing of the gospel is defective without a place for signs and wonders. In effect, as we have already seen, the gospel is 'robbed of its power'.

It is this belief alone that gives the Vineyard Movement its true distinctive. It does not rest on the oft asserted view that its emphasis on prayer for healing is a central distinctive. This is simply untrue – I know many Churches, including my own, who pray for the sick, by name, every week and through the week. No, the Vineyard Movement can only be assessed in the light of its insistence on the centrality of signs and wonders to the gospel. Without this central doctrine the theology of the Vineyard Movement stands or falls.

As we have already seen, the Bible is clear – *only apostles can perform signs and wonders*. In his book *The Toronto Blessing: A Renewal From God? (Volume 1 – Historical Perspectives)* Gary McHale critiques John Wimber's theology stated in *Power Evangelism*. McHale points out that Wimber draws on the writings of great Church figures to make out a case for the concurrence of signs and wonders today. He points out that Wimber quotes Augustine's *City Of God* only in part, in the process giving completely the reverse meaning to the one intended by Augustine:

"Why, they say, are those miracles, which you affirm were wrought formerly, wrought no longer? (Wimber stops here and says that Augustine states that these miracles are 'absolutely trustworthy'. The following is Augustine's response.) I might, indeed, reply that miracles were necessary before the world believed, in order that it might believe. And whoever now-a-days demands to see prodigies that he may believe, is himself a prodigy, because he does not believe when the whole world does......How is it that in enlightened times, in which every impossibility is rejected, the world has, *without any miracles* (note this – *without any miracles* – PG) believed things marvellously incredible....."

Wimber quotes Augustine again: **"For even now miracles are wrought in the name of Christ, whether by His sacraments or by the prayers or relics of His saints;**

(Wimber ends here but Augustine continues), but they are not so brilliant and conspicuous as to cause them to be published with such glory as accompanied the former miracles. For the canon of the sacred writings, which behoved to be closed, cause those to be everywhere recited, and to sink into the memory of all the congregations; but these modern miracles are scarcely known even to the whole population in the midst of which they are wrought, and at best are confined to one spot. For frequently they are known only to a very few persons, while all the rest are ignorant of them." [6]

In short, Wimber has grossly misrepresented Augustine. Augustine was making out a case against those who disbelieved the miracles wrought by the hands of Jesus and the apostles. He specifically points out that such miracles no longer take place *other than through normal prayer and sacraments and relics*. Leaving aside the problems evangelicals would have with sacraments and relics, Augustine clearly does not allow for any miracles wrought by the hands of men. As McHale points out, Wimber goes on to list examples of healings from Augustine. What Wimber completely misses, however, is that Augustine is supporting the supernatural acts of God, none of which were performed at the hands of a living wonder-worker or signs and wonders agent. As McHale says, "After all (this is) John Wimber's whole theology – that gifts continued after the apostolic age."

Wimber and other Vineyard Movement leaders, along with many other signs and wonders friends, often attempt to make out a case for the continuation of these sign-gifts by dragging into their argument the names of some of the great saints of the Church age. In doing so, however, they usually do them a grave disservice, dishonestly perverting the words of some of the fathers of the Church on the issue. The impression we are left with is that they too professed the belief that signs and wonders are contemporary in all ages of the church. Jonathan Edwards is one such name. It brings a whole new dimension of understanding to know that Jonathan Edwards was a cessationist. He believed and stated that the miraculous gifts, ie: those given to men, had ceased. Read for yourself:

"The apostle (Paul) speaks of these gifts of inspiration as childish things in comparison to the influence of the Spirit in divine love: things given to the church only to support it in its minority, till the church should have a complete standing rule established, and all the ordinary means of grace should be settled; but as things that should cease as the church advanced to the state of manhood." And looking ahead to the future of the church: "Therefore I do not expect a restoration of these miraculous gifts in the approaching glorious times of the church, nor do I desire it. It appears to me that it would add nothing to the glory of those times, but rather diminish from it."[7] Hardly the words of a man who believed contemporary signs and wonders were to be sought. We need not stop with Edwards either. We can add virtually every illustrious name used by God throughout the history of the Church: Spurgeon, Luther, Calvin, Augustine and George Whitefield – all cessationists. Even John Wesley was no advocate of signs and wonders wrought through the hands of men. On the other hand, we could of course misrepresent them, these great Christian men – as the advocates of modern signs and wonders do.

Wimber does the same hatchet-job on other historical figures. He describes Montanus and the Montanist movement he spawned, along with Tertullian, one of its leading lights, as proof that miracle-working (ie through men) was still abundant in the early Church. What he does not tell his readers is that both Montanus and Tertullian were condemned as heretics by the extremely biblical early Church for their beliefs and practices, which centred on – you've guessed it – *the continuance of signs and wonders.*

Interestingly, it is the very manner in which Montanus prophesied that led to his condemnation for heresy. It was the loss of self-control by the prophet or his two prophetesses (Priscilla and Maximilia), together with speaking in strange tongues, that was rejected. He was accused of filling these two women 'with the bastard spirit'. Montanus believed he had the ability to anoint others and impart spiritual gifts – remember, the mark of an apostle. Now where have we heard that recently?

An even lengthier history of the Church and its occasional rash of wonder-workers would only prove more of the same. Clearly neither Scripture nor Church history supports the case for a continuation of the phenomena of signs and wonders (note – I am not referring to God's miraculous sovereign interventions) after the time of the apostles. That is, no one since those times has had the manifested ability to perform signs and wonders. We are called to remember and believe what God has done and to witness and be a living testimony to the truth of the gospel. Too many have a theology that stems from the day of Pentecost, with its spectacular events, instead of from the Cross of Calvary. Jesus' work was completed at the Cross, not at Pentecost. Christians are called to pick up their own cross and follow the path of Jesus and the faithful apostles. That is true Christianity – not the pale imitation that seeks a quick-fix for all our ills, that needs the spectacular to be able to prove to the world that God is God. All of us should be working for a true spirituality, seeking the real power of the Spirit to empower change in us and others. The Church does not need to return to its babyhood, a time when it needed the direct revelation of God's power to attest the words of truth spoken by the apostolic company to an unbelieving world.

The Need For Spiritual Discernment

Many evangelicals and others today are falling prey to a major error which is, in turn, leading to others. They are submitting to the growing delusion that focuses on the Holy Spirit instead of Jesus Christ. Nowhere in the Scriptures do Jesus or the disciples pray to the Holy Spirit. The Holy Spirit is truly One Person of the Godhead – but His sole object is to draw us to Jesus. Any Christian path that focuses solely on the Holy Spirit can only lead Christians astray and into mysticism. Why? Because it is the teachings of Christ alone that help us to understand our faith. And Scripture is where we find them. The Holy Spirit then helps us to 'live out' (empowers) our understanding in practice. A Christian life based on worship of the Holy Spirit alone is described well by Michael Horton, "It is the theology of the blowing wind, rather than the dripping blood." [8] Let it be said loud and clear: *the purpose of the Holy Spirit is not to draw us to Him, his sole purpose is to point us to the Person and work of Jesus Christ.*

Think about it for a moment. How is it possible to focus purely on the Holy Spirit? Try to do so without becoming increasingly mystical and (practically and theologically) drifting off into the stratosphere. A worldly analogy would be the equivalent of night lights illuminating an office block. No one concentrates on the lights – everyone concentrates on the building. *That is the function of the lights.* (Remember Mark Haville's points about the nature of songs without doctrinal content, featureless and vague leading to mindlessness?). None of us has a 'low view of the work of the Holy Spirit'. He is the third Person of the indivisible Godhead. But, each of us has a duty to listen to the Scriptures which alone describe His function in justification and sanctification. To understand the nature and purpose of His work is to better understand the doctrine of the Trinity. So many heresies have arisen from a misunderstanding of this doctrine.

Now think about Jesus – it is difficult to do so without thinking about Him, what He did, what He said etc. In short, focusing on the Holy Spirit will produce mindlessness, focusing on our Lord directs us to His teaching and to our understanding of it. Jesus Himself said it, "When the Helper comes...He will testify of Me." (John 15:26)

I have laboured this point because many evangelicals are in danger of grieving the very Spirit they are worshipping because they refuse to understand His role. The abiding concern of all four authors and the main reason for this book is to speak the truth in love. But speaking the truth, of necessity, means refuting error. This fact runs all through the teachings of the New Testament writers. We have become weak in this discipline and we are now reaping the reward – spiritual confusion. Consider the vast space given in the NT to warnings about error, false prophets, 'wolves in sheep's clothing' etc. Look at the whole structure of a book like 2 Peter. Peter is clearly concerned for the *purity* of the true gospel – that we in the Church accept no fakes. And there are plenty around. Which Jesus do you believe in? – the Jesus of Islam? – the Jesus of the Mormons? – the gospel of the Jehovah's Witnesses? – the gospel of universalism? We are specifically called to the gospel and the Jesus witnessed to us *in the writings of the Scriptures*. 2 Peter makes that clear. Peter's concern is to guard the truth – as revealed through Jesus' own words and through the teaching of the apostles. Variations are clearly unacceptable to him. There is no softly, softly approach here towards those *inside* the believing community who would 'secretly introduce destructive heresies.' (2 Peter 2:1) Peter describes such men as 'presumptuous, self-willed... not afraid to speak evil of dignitaries...like natural brute beasts made to be caught and destroyed.' (2 Peter 2:10-12) Clearly, there is no room here for variant gospels.

Paul, Jude and others all had a major concern for pure doctrine – doctrine illuminated by the Spirit. They knew only too well that Christianity *is* lived doctrine. As Paul tells us, "We are called to worship in Spirit and in Truth". Many today are happy to pursue the former (in Spirit) but have no concept of the latter (in Truth). What else does that mean but *obeying what God has told us*. The reverse must also be true – it is exceedingly difficult, if not impossible, to worship God 'in the Spirit' unless we accept His Truth. That means believing the Jesus and the gospel revealed to us through His own Word with all of the teachings (doctrines and clear commandments) that go with it.

Legalism, I hear some shout! And this is where many Christians and Christian leaders today are failing to understand. As we have already seen, we are no longer justified by living according to the law – we are justified by faith alone. But, having been justified with God, are we then free to do as we want? Or, through love and faith, will we want instead to obey our Lord? To please Him will mean obeying His commands – not out of duty but out of love.

Jesus certainly wiped away the Jewish ceremonial laws through His atonement on the Cross, but He Himself said, "Do not think that I came to destroy the Law or the Prophets. I did not come to destroy but to fulfil. For assuredly, I say to you, till heaven and earth pass away, one jot or one tittle will by no means pass from the law till all is fulfilled...Whoever therefore breaks one of the least of these commandments, and teaches men so, shall be called least in the kingdom of heaven, but whoever does and teaches them, he shall be called great in the kingdom of heaven." (Matthew 5:17-19)

This, in my view, is one of the major misunderstandings in the Church in our age; there is growing confusion over the areas of grace and law. It is certainly poorly taught in our Churches. We are free – but now that we have our freedom, what would we do with it? If God would have us obey His teachings, then surely we should prove our love to Him by our obedience. Let me say again, we are no longer justified by the law, only by faith. But God's eternal laws, now written on our hearts, can still guide us. We seek His ways not out of duty , but out of love for Him. By following this ancient path we will be sanctified.

Listen to Jesus, "He who has My commandments and keeps them, it is he who loves Me." (John 14:21) And again, "If anyone loves Me, he will keep My word...He who does not love Me does not keep My words." (John 14:23-24) And again, "Sanctify them by Your truth; Your word is truth." (John 17:17). The fact is, it is not possible to worship our God as He wills it, unless we understand the truth – and the truth is found in God's authoritative Word *alone*. We can trust it and we are able to judge (spiritually discern) by it.

The truth in our day and age is that the Church is desperately short of one vastly important gift – the gift of spiritual discernment. In emphasising the Spirit over the Word, our signs and wonders friends are treading the path of an ancient heresy: mystic gnosticism. It is our hope that this book will sound alarm bells among some of those brothers and sisters in the faith. All four authors would say, "You need not listen to us – so long as you listen to God's Word. *There* is real truth." Test what you hear, test what you see by that. Phenomena alone is *never* self-authenticating.

The problem with gnosticism as Pastor Bill Randles points out is that it is "notoriously antinomian (anti-law). Gnostics believe that because of their mystical knowledge which has helped them escape the material world, they are not under any law at all. There are no moral obligations for them, they are 'free in Christ'." Randles quotes 1 John 2:3-5: "And hereby we do know that we know Him, if we keep His commandments. He that saith, I know Him, and keepeth not His commandments, is a liar, and the truth is not in him. But whoso keepeth His word, in him verily is the love of God perfected; hereby we know that we are in Him."

Randles goes on, " John is telling us not to be confused, it's not that salvation is by the law: it isn't. But if you really have been saved, and love God, you'll be concerned about His commandments, but out of love, not duty! I don't care one lick about Jewish ceremonial law or food laws, but I am deeply concerned about the ten commandments which shall never pass away." [9]

All of this is highly relevant to our signs and wonders friends with their pursuing of new revelation – support for which is not in the Scriptures. It directly bears upon ways of thinking about healing, spiritual warfare techniques, occultish 'visualisation' techniques in prayer, and for attempting to resurrect the offices of apostles and prophets – which simply have no place in today's Church.

Aha, you say, but God could be doing something new in the end-times before Jesus returns, ie: post-Scripture! If He is doing so, then clearly God got it wrong when He revealed to us the nature of the end-time right up to the reappearance and second coming of our Lord. We are not promised new apostles and prophets, neither are we promised new revelation (new teachings). The only thing we are consistently told is to trust and obey Him and that we show we love Him by our obedience. In doing so we would be witnesses to the world until Jesus returns.

Where Are We Going?

The significant thinking behind modern signs and wonders is a reflection of a theology called 'Dominionism'–better known in Britain as 'Restorationism'. Most Christians are not aware of this. Sadly, all too many are falling (often literally) under the influence of Christian leaders who believe aspects of these theologies. They themselves have no idea of what they are involved in – certainly their leaders will not tell them. Put simply, these theologies believe that the Church is going to be made a strong powerful force in the world. The precursor to this is the rediscovery or putting back in the Church (restoration) the more spectacular gifts (signs and wonders) to be performed through the hands of new end-time prophets and apostles (restored gifts, restored offices in the Church). Instead of relying on the doctrines of the faith, the Church will then be able to visibly unify, not around doctrines which are clearly divisive, but around sensual 'experiences of God'. Ecumenical unity, as you can see, is on virtually everybody's agenda. The only casualty in all this is Truth. The Scriptures make a nonsense of all of it.

As the massive worldwide Church then becomes unified, its political influence will grow and it will draw people to it through it's spectacular shows of power. The ultimate goal is to dominate through world government (this is Dominionism). For an in-depth approach to what many in today's Church are working towards, both at Government level and in the Church, read US researcher Al Dager's excellent 'Vengeance Is Ours.'[10]

Now, whether you find all that too hard to take in or not does not matter for our purpose here. What matters is that the only reference to signs and wonders in the last days in the pages of Scripture, is to warnings about lying signs and wonders and false prophets. Many of these are already talking in apocalyptic terms of 'the revival of all revivals', 'a powerful Church', 'reclaiming God's world from Satan', 'pulling down strongholds' etc. You may be very familiar with the language – this jargon is their hallmark.

The Scriptures on the other hand call us to take up our cross, to be faithful and, most significantly, to suffer as our Lord suffered. This is not popular theology with our signs and wonders friends. "Follow me" was Jesus call. His oath took Him to the Cross. Our signs and wonders friends want a powerful Church to allow us to swagger through life thrusting our fists into the air claiming victory – in God's name.

It should come as no surprise then that God foresaw all this. He knew that truth would always be hard to accept – even for many who had turned to His Son. Where are we going? Well, Scripture is only too clear – before Jesus returns the Church is headed for the greatest apostasy in its history. It will not be through attacks from outside the Church, either. The danger is from within. It is from a pseudo-Christian spirituality that will deceive many. Satan's greatest work will not be achieved by Islam or any other religion – that would be too obvious an approach. His greatest work will be to achieve a counterfeit Christianity based on the ancient heresy of mystical gnosticism, steeped in power theology and power-working lying signs and wonders. In fact, we are told, it will get so bad for true believers that Jesus will have to return to 'save the remnant'. How do we know...?

"Don't let anyone deceive you in any way, for that day (ie the day Jesus returns) will not come until the *rebellion* (Greek word *apostasia*: apostasy) occurs and the man of lawlessness is revealed, the man doomed to destruction (2 Thessalonians 2:3.)

"The coming of the lawless one will be in accordance with the work of Satan in all kinds of counterfeit miracles, signs and wonders, and in every sort of evil that deceives those who are perishing. They perish because they refuse to love the truth and so be saved. For this reason God sends them a powerful delusion so that they will believe the lie and so that all will be condemned who have not believed the truth but have delighted in wickedness." (2 Thessalonians 2:9-12)

Either the rash of end-time prophets and our signs and wonders friends are right or the Scriptures are right – both cannot be.

In this book you have heard from Mark who performed many of the signs and wonders that occur in today's Church. His life was transformed by the truth of God's Word. Many are confused today because they are bemused by what they see. They see 'things happening', ie: phenomena. Philip Foster's section of this book answers a significant question of many: if it is not God, then how is it done? You know now that many alleged signs and wonders are simply a learned process – shamans, occultists and modern day hypnotists use *all* the same techniques. As Mark Haville points out: he did it, you could do it, anyone could do it.

The 'atmosphere creators' have simply taken these ancient techniques they have stumbled on and brought them into the Church. Why? Because as the American TV evangelist Benny Hinn points out, "It works!" Of course 'it works' – it always has. And new movements, based on these practices, are now becoming increasingly rampant *inside* the Church. We have heard much about the so-called 'fruit' of the Toronto Experience from Chris Hand – at the centre of things when Toronto hit the UK. And finally, we have looked again at the Scriptures.

In all of this, never did we need the gift of spiritual discernment more. Even this is seen by many as some kind of mystical gift, given only to a precious few 'anointed' ones. They are quite wrong. Our Lord was true to His word, we have not been left 'as orphans'. The Scriptures give us everything we need to help us discern truth. All of the writers here believe God is testing His Church in our day – to see if we are prepared to hold to His truth and to confirm that we still have the stomach to actively contend for the gospel and refute error. "...the goal of Christian mission is not success, but faithful witness; not power, but proclamation; not technique, but truth; not method, but message." [11]

Charles Spurgeon, that great preacher of the Word of God, was told that some were supposedly bent on restoring the miracle-working gifts of the apostles in his day. He responded cryptically by observing, "A bottomless pit of fanaticism is yawning." But he did not leave it there – he threw out this challenge to contemporary claimants to apostleship (and we four now echo his words): "The apostles were empowered to do many things, but who are you? Do you claim to be their successors? Then work miracles similar to theirs: take up serpents and drink deadly things without being harmed thereby; prove to us that you have seen the Lord, or even that cloven tongues of fire have sat upon each of you." [12]

In the same book the American author James Montgomery Boice, referring to an oft-misused passage on (real) spiritual warfare says, "Ephesians 6 does not promote miracle-working as the way to do battle against Satan, but instead admonishes us to be clothed with Christ's righteousness and to be armed with 'the sword of the Spirit, which is the Word of God' (v.17). The Spirit's weapon, therefore, is not additional revelations, nor 'power encounters', but the written text of Holy Scripture." [13]

Spurgeon's quote itself echoes the report by Luke of the attempted wonder-working activities of the seven sons of Sceva, a Jewish priest. They were invoking the name of Jesus wrongly and elicited this response: "Jesus I know, and I know about Paul, but who are you?" (Acts 19:13-16)

Unless the Church and its members respond and begin refuting error while preaching the true gospel, many more young and vulnerable Christians are destined to join the leaders of today's signs and wonders movement in their delusion, and in doing so will become embroiled in preaching Paul's "a different gospel – which is really no gospel at all." Let us truly worship Him, as He commands, in Spirit – and in Truth. To God be the glory.

Notes

1 Don Carson, The Purpose of Signs & Wonders in the New Testament from:
Power Religion: The Selling Out of the Evangelical Church pgs. 92/93, Moody Press
2 Ibid pg. 93
3 Michael Horton, Introduction to Power Religion: **The Selling Out of the Evangelical Church** pg. 17, Moody Press
4 Dr Martin Lloyd-Jones, Prove All Things pg. 97/98, Kingsway
5 Walter Chantry, Signs of the Apostles pg. 25, Banner of Truth
6 Gary McHale, The Toronto Blessing: A Renewal From God – Vol 1. Historical Perspectives pg. 54, Canadian Christian Publications
7 Jonathan Edwards, The Distinguishing Marks of A Work Of The Spirit Of God pgs. 139/140
8 Michael Horton, Modern Reformation Magazine.
9 Bill Randles, Making War In The Heavenlies pg. 164 St Matthew's Publications
10. Albert James Dager, Vengeance Is Ours Sword Publications (US)
11. Michael Horton, Power Religion pg. 15, Moody Press.
12. Charles Spurgeon, New Park Street & Metropolitan Volumes (Vol. 30 pg. 11)
13 James Montgomery Boice, Power Religion pg. 123, Moody Press.

Useful addresses:

'Toronto Blessing' Helpline: Chris Hand, PO Box 8400, London SE13 6ZT or on 0181 318 3854

National Prayer Network: Mark Haville, 37 Wykeham Road, Kenton, Harrow, Middlesex HA3 8LL UK. Telephone 07000 073 373. Fax 0181 909 9938.

Christian Research Network (CRN) is contactable by writing to Peter Glover, PO Box 8400, London SE13 6ZT or by e-mail on crn @ukonline.co.uk

For Further Reading:

Christianity In Crisis Hank Hanegraaff, Harvest House ISBN 0-89081-9769

The Great Evangelical Disaster Francis Schaeffer, Kingsway ISBN 0-86065-341-2

Vengeance Is Ours (on Dominionism) Albert James Dager, Sword Publishers ISBN 0-9626632-0-4

Jonathan Edwards On Revival Banner of Truth ISBN 0 85151 431 6

Power Religion: The Selling Out of the Evangelical Church Various: Michael Horton, RC Sproul, Don Carson and others: Moody Press ISBN 1-872059-74-0

The Seduction of Christianity: Spiritual Discernment In The Last Days, Dave Hunt & T.A. McMahon Harvest House ISBN 0-89081-441-4

The Strength of Weakness: Roy Clements, Christian Focus Publications ISBN 1-85792-073-2

Hypnosis And The Christian: Martin & Deidre Bobgan, Bethany House ISBN 0-87123-402-5